MW01462516

Jesus Before Christendom

Frederico Pereira da Silva Júnior

By the Spirit
Francisco Leite de Bittencourt Sampaio

1898

KNOWSPIRITISM
KNOW SPIRITISM, KNOW THYSELF

Translated from the Portuguese original
"Jesus Perante a Cristandade"
7ª Edição, FEB, 1975

All rights reserved.

ISBN: 9798316296866

JESUS BEFORE CHRISTENDOM

Francisco Leite de Bittencourt Sampaio invites readers to rediscover Christ in the pure light of His original message—free from centuries of dogma. Dictated through the mediumship of Frederico Pereira da Silva Júnior, Jesus Before Christendom traces the Master's life from birth to resurrection, illuminating vital questions of faith and elaborating on the constitution of His physical body.

Across eleven engaging chapters, Bittencourt Sampaio explores timeless Gospel themes—God as Spirit, true baptism, and the merciful essence of the Creator—while warning of distortions that have crept into Christ's teachings. He calls believers to return to the heart of the Good News "in spirit and truth," offering a deeper understanding of the Divine Master's life and words.

Both a historical reflection and a spiritual manifesto, Jesus Before Christendom transcends institutions and creeds, guiding seekers toward a living encounter with Christ's transformative message—still powerful for humanity's spiritual evolution.

CONTENTS

NOTICE   1

PREFACE   3

CHAPTER I   6
In the beginning was the Word, and the Word was with God, and the Word was God. — The Word was made flesh. — Zechariah's speechlessness; John's birth. — True baptism. — God is spirit. — Paradise, Hell, and Purgatory. — The apparent body of the Divine Master. — The angel Gabriel's greeting and annunciation to the Most Holy Virgin.

CHAPTER II   15
The birth of the Divine Master. — Songs heard by the shepherds. — Moses crosses the Red Sea. — The golden calf. — Moses orders the great slaughter.

CHAPTER III   20
Passover festivities. — Jesus among the doctors. — The baptism of Jesus. — Confession. — The arrest and death of the Forerunner. — The beheading of the innocents. — Original sin. — John the Baptist, the reincarnation of Elijah. — The temptation of the Divine Master in the desert by the devil.

CHAPTER IV   30
The wedding at Cana. — Jesus expels the merchants from the

temple. — The market of the sacraments. — Spiritism is the
forerunner of the Spirit of Truth. — Nicodemus's question to the
Divine Master. — The law of reincarnation. — Hell. — Tenants of
the Lord's Vineyard. — The resurrection of the Spirit. — Jesus and
the Samaritan woman.

CHAPTER V 43
Jesus is the resurrection and the life. — The cure of the paralytic by
the Pool of Bethesda. — The Sabbath day according to Mosaic law.
— True fasting. — The multiplication of the loaves and fishes.

CHAPTER VI 51
The flesh and blood of Our Lord Jesus Christ. — Promises and
offerings according to the Church of Rome. — The parable of the
barren fig tree. — The oath before the Gospel. — The Syllabus. —
Idolatry. — The succession to the chair of St. Peter. — The
commerce of images. — Burying the dead is a duty for the dead. —
The intolerance of the Roman Church.

CHAPTER VII 64
Spiritism in the light of the Gospels. — The law of reincarnation.
— The eternity of punishment, according to the Church of Rome.
— The Great King's feast. — Anathemas of the Catholic Church.
— The parables of the adulterous woman and the prodigal son. —
The Lord's Prayer. — Marriage and celibacy.

CHAPTER VIII 74
True death: the death of the Spirit. — Lazarus's illness; his
apparent death and resurrection. — The scribes and Pharisees, on
the advice of Caiaphas, decide to kill Jesus. — The Divine Master's
entry into Jerusalem.

CHAPTER IX 79
The Paschal Supper. — The Eucharist. — Jesus washes the feet of
His disciples. — The prediction of Judas's betrayal. — The many
mansions in the Father's House. — The Consoler. — Jesus
predicts to Peter that he will deny Him three times.

CHAPTER X 87
The kiss of betrayal. — Peter cuts off Malchus's ear. — The three
denials by the Apostle of Faith. — Pilate's efforts to free the

Divine Lord. — Judas's remorse. — Words of the Gentle Lamb to the daughters of Jerusalem. — Calvary. — The words of Jesus to the Most Holy Virgin and to the Beloved Disciple. — The last words of the Divine Master. — Nicodemus and Joseph of Arimathea place Jesus's body in the tomb.

CHAPTER XI 95

The visit of the pious women to the holy sepulcher. — The appearance of the Divine Master to Mary Magdalene. — Magdalene, by the Lord's command, tells the disciples of His resurrection. — The appearance of the Divine Master to His disciples. — Thomas's disbelief. — Jesus appears again to His disciples, in Thomas's presence. — The words of the Divine Lord to the Apostle of Faith. — The Lord's Ascension — The Consoler among men — The Spiritist Doctrine.

LAST WORDS 105

ABOUT THE AUTHORS 108

"EVERY PLANT WHICH MY HEAVENLY FATHER HAS NOT PLANTED SHALL BE UPROOTED."
— MATTHEW, CHAPTER XV, VERSE 13.

NOTICE

This work represents the sweet fruit, gathered by humble workers in the holy vineyard of the Beloved Master, through His divine mercy. In special sessions held over six months, attended by the brothers and friends who, under the protection of the good Guide Ismael, study the HOLY GOSPELS, we received it through our good companion Frederico Pereira da Silva Júnior, who lent his somnambulistic medium's apparatus to the devoted servant of the Lord who dictated it to him, transmitting these pages radiant with light and truth. They arrive to bring the Christian world faith and hope in the mercy of Our Lord Jesus Christ, who descends upon the poor exiles on Earth by allowing them the knowledge of the truths contained in the Divine Code.

It fell to me to arrange the received communications for publication, because of the undeserved choice that enlightened spirit—who not so long ago was also our work companion on Earth—made of me. I strove, imploring the help of my good Guide and my protectors in the beyond, and employing the best effort my poor spirit could muster, to fulfill that lofty task which, by the Lord's divine mercy alone, was assigned to me.

I kiss the generous and kind hand that reached out to me, leading me to the work of the holy field. May Jesus, our Divine Master and Lord, fill with grace and blessings the good laborer of His holy vineyard, and from the height of His glory cast a look of mercy and forgiveness upon this wretched sinner who, still clothed in the rags of his moral and intellectual poverty, endeavored to serve His faithful disciple.

May you find in these sublime pages, reader, comfort for your sorrows, and, by meditating upon the divine truths they unveil for you, may you behold the most sacred image of our Divine Redeemer, just as He is and as the HOLY GOSPELS present Him to us.

Such are the wishes of the least among your brothers in Our Lord Jesus Christ.

— Pedro Luiz de Oliveira Sayão
August – 1898.

PREFACE

To you, oh Most Holy Virgin! Sovereign of the Heavens! Mystical Rose, in whose bosom all misfortune finds shelter; to you, hope of the afflicted, soul of charity, to you I dedicate this first endeavor I make, after my passing, to bear witness to Our Lord Jesus Christ of the greatness of my gratitude for the many mercies He surrounded me with on Earth, causing the seeds of the Gospel to sprout within my human breast, to germinate and ripen to eternal life.

To you, oh Holy Virgin, all my devotion in, rising up from the solitude of the grave, emerging again by the grace of the Eternal, to show your most Beloved Son Jesus, Our Lord, before Christendom.

Glory, glory to you, Immaculate Virgin Mother!

To my brothers on Earth, to those in whose souls a blossom of hope still thrives; to my brothers on Earth, whose Spirits still flounder in the waters of that tremendous flood of errors, crimes, and uncertainties; to those who, clinging to branches of coral, watch the divine seeding swept away in torrents by those who took upon themselves the greatest responsibilities before their Creator and their Divine Master; to my brothers on Earth, to those who, in that immense desert of the world, listen for the voices of heaven, seeking earnestly the star that leads them to a new Canaan, I dedicate this most humble work that has no other purpose but to share with suffering humanity the spiritual bread I received from Our Lord Jesus Christ, through the grace of His love and mercy.

Jesus Before Christendom

Yes; because, although His doctrine was preached twenty centuries ago and sealed with His priceless blood, the peoples of Earth still do not know the true Jesus; they still do not know His true doctrine, nor do they practice His true teachings. Those who took up the task to make Him known to humanity have segregated Him, cloaking Him in the thick shadows of errors and crimes, such that the Gentle Lamb, the Divine Son of God, cannot be seen by His brothers on Earth, nor can His sweet and persuasive word penetrate into consciences locked tight, barred by the hands of those who should have been the first to grant them full openness, so that they might comprehend all His truth.

How shall we find Jesus? Where shall we feel the vibration of His most sacred words, if, by the Gospel, we see Him in hovels, in humble huts, aflame with fervor, calling the creature to its Creator, whereas today we are invited to see the Nazarene—and the reproduction of His words—in the ostentation of palaces that rise in all the cities of the world, which, as an affront to the founder of Christianity, are called God's Church?

Centuries of struggles! And when we hoped to see human conscience awaken to an understanding of its God, we find ourselves forced once again to reproduce the inscription from the façade of the temple at Delphi: Man, know thyself!

The blood shed on the cross has become the lake in which humanity drowns in despair, failing to understand that, by gushing forth, it was meant to bring peace, love, and human fellowship.

The world is a desert where Jesus cannot be found, where Achilles still rules over consciences. Jesus remains the despised, and, after so many struggles, man still does not understand that Earth is a winter station where the Spirit comes to prepare for the springtime of heaven!

And after so many struggles, after so many palaces have been raised to which humankind is summoned for the sacraments, humanity still asks, like the great governor of Judea: What is truth?

And it is right to ask, for truth is Jesus, and humanity does not know Jesus! But the time draws near; that thick veil covering the true image of our Divine Master will be torn down the middle by the Spirit of Truth. Then, you who let yourselves be lulled by nothing but the affairs of the world; you, successors of Peter, who replaced his humble pilgrim's staff with a king's scepter; you, pontiffs who have transformed the House of God into a market of consciences, shall behold in all His splendor the one rejected by all ages, Jesus of Nazareth, the firstborn of the Most High!

The Spirit of Truth, Himself sending His envoys to Earth to kindle in consciences the love of His and our God, the love for all God's creatures, shall pronounce the final word to the tribes of Israel dispersed throughout the universe, calling them to redemption and repentance.

Following the biblical texts, studying the words of the prophets, of Jesus and His apostles, we will make the Divine Nazarene reappear in human conscience. This is our effort and, for that, oh my God, my Creator and Father, I ask You for the inspiration of my elders, for all the light of Your infinite mercy, and for the goodwill of those who must accompany me along this shadowy and thorny path, until we find Your Most Beloved Son, so that we may show Him as He truly is to the eyes of Christendom.

CHAPTER I

In the beginning was the Word, and the Word was with God and the Word was God. — The Word became flesh. — The muteness of Zechariah; the birth of John. — True baptism. — God is spirit. — Paradise, Hell, and Purgatory. — The apparent body of the Divine Master. — The greeting and announcement of the angel Gabriel to the Most Holy Virgin[1].

Moses, speaking to a people poor in mentality yet rich in passions, prone to stray from the path traced out by the Lord and needing to be given knowledge of the origin of things, wrote Genesis, which is found in the Old Testament.

The people for whom he legislated were weak and incapable of understanding the higher role played by the Earth in the hierarchy of worlds. Thus, to satisfy the needs of their minds, he presented Earth as the general principle of the entire universe.

Sensing and feeling the fierceness of men's instincts, he wrote Leviticus as though it were the entrance to a great dike capable of holding back the invasive wave of their evils, which would carry their Spirits to the depths of the most terrible abysses of perdition. These were laws suited to the environment in which he acted as judge, as the leader of an army of Spirits fallen from the purity, from the innocence, from which they had departed.

---

[1] Original publisher's note: John, Chapter I; Luke, Chapter I; Malachi, Chapter IV, verses 5 to 6; Deuteronomy, Chapter XVIII, verses 15 to 18; and Isaiah, Chapters XL, verse 3 and IX, verse 2, whose complete texts the reader will find in their copy of the Bible, thus allowing us to reduce the dimensions of this volume. —Brazilian Spiritist Federation (FEB), 1975.

Today, however, since the human spirit has developed, man tears open the bosom of Nature and goes out into infinite space in search of a series of worlds sustained there by the attraction of the universal fluid. Today, as intelligence better grasps the reason behind things, we, by the will and by the grace of Our Lord Jesus Christ, can, within the words of His Gospel, help you understand its principle, even though we are still unable to grasp or declare the whole truth.

In the beginning was the Word, and the Word was with God and the Word was God.

In the beginning, that is, before the existence of the planet you inhabit, Jesus, the Purest Spirit, the Father's firstborn, took from the scattered elements, condensed by the universal fluid, and formed a great incandescent sphere which, obeying the eternal laws of the gravitation of bodies, described its orbit around a great star.

Surrounded by great vapors due to the high temperature, it rose into the heights and, through the power of His will, He gathered those two elements that Earth's science calls hydrogen and oxygen, thereby producing water.

Over the course not of six days, but over the course of centuries, the sphere gradually cooled, and the liquid materials contained within its core, in their attempt—through boiling—to breach the crust of that same sphere, produced the irregularities observed on the planet's surface.

With the temperature's drop, the waters fell as rain and, obeying the laws of gravitation, sought out the lower basins of the sphere, forming the seas.

Corrosive materials, together with the waters, eroded and bore toward the great basins the debris torn from the peaks, forming sedimentary layers. And after many centuries of further transformations, by the will and governance of Jesus, in those sedimentary layers there appeared humus which, saturated with carbonic acid, enabled the first lilies to bloom, the first palm tree to rise.

Thus, in my humble understanding, the exile of Earth was organized; thus was organized the planet of atonement, where Spirits who had strayed from love of their God come to take on bodies so that they may suffer, so that they may taste death and then rise again to life.

In the beginning was the Word, the Word was with God and the Word was God.

Let us understand this expression.

The Word, according to the Beloved Disciple in his Divine Epic, is nothing but the will and the utterance of the Eternal.

Jesus perceived the will of His Creator and Father and was, through His word, the transmitter of that will in the presence of all Nature.

In the beginning was the Word. Yes.

At the beginning of the creation of planet Earth, Jesus, we may say, God's medium, carried out the will of His Creator in the whole of creation. And the Word became flesh, and dwelt among us — and the Word became body, and that body dwelt among us — and Jesus took on a heavenly body, in the words of the great Apostle to the Gentiles, and came to dwell among men, fulfilling the prophecies, offering them the means of salvation in exchange for His precious blood.

As the time of His appearance on Earth drew near, there was a great priest named Zechariah, husband of Elizabeth, she who deemed herself barren.

While Zechariah was in the temple, exercising his ministry, he received, as the clairvoyant and clairaudient medium that he was, the manifestation of a great Spirit who told him that from Elizabeth's womb would come the great Prophet of the Lord.

Zechariah, despite being a believer, despite being consciously aware that the will of God is carried out irrespective of all circumstances and all considerations entertained by men, doubted, because his unfortunate Elizabeth bore the mark of her disgrace: she was advanced in years and was barren.

The Angel of the Lord, to give him proof of the truth of his words, added: You shall become mute until the day when this event that I now reveal to you is fulfilled; until the moment when you are called to name the child, who, I tell you in advance, should be called John.

Zechariah's vocal organs were thus paralyzed by the magnetic fluid, and in fact, it was only at the moment when they were deciding on the name that would be given to the innocent babe that Zechariah recovered his voice. That is, the Spirits removed the paralyzing magnetic fluids, and when they handed him the tablet on which he was to record this name, he wrote on it, saying: John is his name.

This event, which filled Elizabeth's household with joy—this phenomenon, in human terms, which lifted the Lord's servant from disgrace—was, in the eyes of the strong, a condemnation, a painful suffering for the great priest Zechariah, for he remained speechless for quite some time.

But what of faith and the love of sacred matters?! Indeed, can the sufferings we endure, by the grace granted us by the Lord, be greater than the sacrifices of the idolaters, who offered themselves to be crushed beneath the wheels of the great chariot of Siva[2] and other idols, without any true object of belief and solely to please a fiction?

No, certainly not. That suffering was a joy for Zechariah, who, filled with humility, endured that paralysis while waiting for the word of the Lord to be fulfilled in his house.

Thus, the voice of one crying in the wilderness was already in the world; upon Earth's surface appeared the great prophet of the Nazarene, preparing the way for His evangelical passage.

John, grown to manhood, sought out the deserts; as all prophets do, he prepared his Spirit in the bosom of Nature and then traveled throughout the tribes of Israel, preaching words of hope and repentance, summoning peoples to penitence, so they might receive the Great Envoy.

He was the voice of one crying in the wilderness, seeking out the banks of the vast Jordan, inviting the people to come receive the waters of baptism, that is, to commune with him in the God he announced.

Presenting a rite meant to replace, from the outset, one that no longer had a reason to exist—namely circumcision, the sign of the covenant between God and His creatures, which, though originally employed as a sign of conversion of Spirits to the laws of Jehovah[3], was in that region, nevertheless, a hygienic necessity due to the scorching climate—John instituted baptism by pouring water on the heads of men.

Those who heard his words, who perceived the truths he spoke, who repented and accepted his doctrine, that is, the doctrine of Jesus, were baptized by him. Thus, each person bore the responsibility for his or her own act; feeling and reasoning, they were in a position to accept or reject the doctrine that was preached to them. Since their free will was respected, they could act and decide by their own will. This, Christians in Christ, is true baptism.

And is the baptism of today—the one that is offered throughout

---

[2] A Hindu god, the third person of the Indian trinity; a god who transforms and creates by means of death; who kills to create. His worshippers, the Shaivites, consider him the greatest of gods, and there was a time in Ceylon and Hindustan when they regarded him as the one supreme god. He dwells on Mount Kailasa, which is why he is also called Gandhara (he who carries the Ganges on his head), since the Ganges descends from the slopes of Mount Kailasa, the god's abode.

[3] "He who exists by Himself": one of the names by which the Israelites refer to God.

Christendom—the baptism of John?

Certainly not. It is not the baptism practiced by Our Lord Jesus Christ, who presented Himself to the great prophet so that, in communion with the repentant, He might obey the will of His Father, the will of His Creator.

What, then?! You take a child that does not think, a little one that does not reason, and baptize it, and in the full nineteenth century, you command that someone else decide which religion he or she should adopt—and then believe that, by a mere external ceremony, you have made that child a Christian in Christ, only to judge tomorrow that this person is an apostate?

Do you take that child into your care, instill in its Spirit a sense of religion?

Do you, perhaps, follow its steps, guiding it like a pilgrim toward light and truth, never letting it wander from your example, an example which should be those of Our Lord Jesus Christ and His apostles?

Where and when do you act thus? That is what, throughout this present work, we will seek to determine, not in order to arouse the anger of believers against you, but rather to beg for their compassion, their mercy, for, constituting yourselves as representatives of Our Lord Jesus Christ on Earth—aside from the exception of a few illustrious men who knew how to honor their ministry—you neither perform the works of Jesus Christ nor strive to follow the luminous path of the apostles, when they went forth in the name of their Divine Master, from tribe to tribe, from city to city, bearing the word of love, charity, and salvation.

If belief and faith demand freedom, reason, and will—freedom for action, intelligence for reasoning, conscience for volition—we cannot comprehend how one can take a little being, devoid of freedom, reason, and will, and impose religious precepts upon it, instilling in its soul the Holy Doctrine of Our Lord Jesus Christ.

When you can show me anything in the biblical text that authorizes you to act in this way, I shall consider myself in error and shall publicly confess it.

So as not to weary your intelligence by searching for the truth, suffice it to consult Matthew, Chapter XXVIII, verse 19, where we find Jesus commanding His disciples to preach His doctrine to all nations, to all peoples, baptizing them in the name of the Father, the Son, and the Holy Spirit.

Note well that preaching precedes baptism.

Therefore, by that teaching, by that command, baptism is nothing more than a symbol that confirms the beliefs embraced by an individual soul before its Creator and Father. But to preach a doctrine to those still wrapped in the swaddling clothes of infancy, to a Spirit unhinged by fear of death (for life on Earth is death to the Spirit), might fulfill the outward forms of baptism, but never its ideal, never its core, never its morality as expressed by the Gospel's teaching.

I know that one day Rome's intolerance will cast anathema on this humble work. But of what importance are anathemas, of what importance are excommunications, when my Spirit feels the necessity of sharing with my brothers and sisters the little it has learned in the beyond, thereby fulfilling the commitments made to Our Lord Jesus Christ in previous existences?

In the beginning was the Word, and the Word was with God and the Word was God. The Word became flesh and dwelt among us. Jesus, taking on an apparently material body, came to be on Earth the Word of God.

Consult the Chaldean paraphrases and you will find, in many passages, the Messiah represented as the Word of God on Earth.

God is spirit; His will is thought. His thought resides in the purest Spirit of Jesus, becomes the Word, and the Word comes to dwell among men, teaching the words of salvation. Thus, just as in man the spoken word results from his will, so in Jesus, by His purity, it resulted from the will of the Father; Jesus is the Word of God, Jesus is the Word.

But the Word became flesh and dwelt among us.

Moses, as I have already mentioned, spoke to a people poor in mentality and rich in material excess.

Laying down laws, he needed to present a beginning accessible to the people for whom he legislated; with this in mind, he put forward Adam as the trunk of the human family.

But since that beginning of creation cannot satisfy the human intelligence today, nor adapt to the progress of the human spirit, which, in its investigations in Geology, Archeology, Astronomy, Chronicles, and History, seeks the probable origin of all things, we must use our reason and intelligence in the light of spiritual truth. In so doing, without destroying the Gospelic principles, we can harmonize everything and satisfy men's eagerness insofar as they are able to bear it.

Once the planet—Earth—was formed, we see in it Paradise, Hell, and Purgatory.

Paradise for the Spirits who, having emigrated from lower worlds, find on Earth, so to speak, their oasis.

Hell for those who, having previously inhabited worlds superior to Earth, descended to it for their pride, their rebellion, their original sins, so that they might undergo trials and thereby return to the paradise they had lost.

Purgatory for Spirits in transition, those who, having attained a certain degree of perfectibility, have become fit to guide humanity.

To make humanity spring from Adam's trunk is not to comprehend God in all His greatness.

We judge that the world was inhabited by colonies of Spirits united according to their leanings, their imperfections, and their levels of progress. Hence the differences in races, in types, in customs, in religions, and in instincts.

How were these colonies organized?

We do not know. Yet it seems to us that the one granted to Abraham was the most advanced, the one made up of Spirits most inclined toward love of their God and love of their neighbor.

If we did not explain matters in this way, philosophers would ask—with complete justification—why Jesus chose to favor the house of Israel above all others. Given that there were other peoples, some intellectually more advanced and some morally more backward, why did all the attention of Our Lord Jesus Christ focus on the house of Jacob?

It seems to us to be because from there, from that blessed trunk, families of Spirits prepared to influence the world and fully grasp the divine truth would come one after another.

Only thus can we also understand the lack of foundation for the story of the tower of Babel, said to cause the confusion of tongues. Tongues were confused by the Spirits themselves, in their own respective colonies.

And the Word became flesh and dwelt among us. Flesh! But there are heavenly bodies and earthly bodies.

Jesus, taking upon Himself the regeneration of humanity, having to confront many societies filled with prejudice, error, and sin—needing to destroy the fanaticism of some, the deism of others, pantheism, and many other sects and philosophical systems that made deep grooves in man's thought in the school of Alexandria, surrounded by this mass of heterogenous elements for the expansion of His Good News—needed to assume the apparent body of man and present Himself to the world in that form.

We do not fully know all the transformations of the fluids, but it appears to us that the Spirits commanded to accompany our Divine Master in His mission on Earth went to gather, from the bloom of the vine and the bloom of the wheat fields, the elements that composed the body of Our Lord Jesus Christ.

To us, who are Spiritists, this is no longer a hypothesis but a perfectly confirmed truth.

A Spirit takes from a flower, causes its molecules to lose cohesion, transforms them into fluids, and, if it so wills, reassembles those same fluids, restores the cohesion of the molecules, and brings the same flower back into being.

The fluid taken from the bloom of the vine and from the bloom of wheat fields was what condensed in the womb of the Most Holy Virgin, giving her the form of pregnancy that so troubled the just man Joseph.

If it is not by the will of man, nor of the flesh, that a Spirit is formed, but by the will of God; if woman's role in gestation is only to bear the body that must house the Spirit who is coming into the world, then logically we affirm that the Virgin Mary was the mother of Our Lord Jesus Christ—that is, she gave Him His body—while always preserving her virginity, by the influence of the Holy Spirit, the phalanx of good Spirits who went to draw from the heart of Nature itself the slender veil of apparent flesh that enveloped the Divine Master, from which He would free Himself by an act of will at moments unwelcome to His final agony.

On a small hill, within a most humble home, the Holy Virgin sat in rapt reflection when she saw before her eyes the angel of the Lord, Gabriel by name, who said to her, greeting her:

— Hail Mary, full of grace, the Lord is with you; blessed are you among women; from your womb shall come the Redeemer of the world, and you shall call His name Jesus.

Mary, emerging from her sweet reverie, replied:

— How can this be, since I know no man?

— Believe, O Holy Virgin! He who shall come from your womb shall be called the Son of God.

— Let it be done in His handmaid according to the Lord's will.

Thus the union of Earth with Heaven was made; the pact of redemption between creature and Creator was sealed.

Finally, the voices of the prophets were to be fulfilled, and the ten tribes of Israel, gathered by Jeroboam[4] and lost to idolatry, were to

---

[4] Author of the schism of the ten tribes. Rehoboam, Solomon's son, having angered the people, ten tribes then abandoned him to choose Jeroboam as ruler; thus he became the first king of Israel. He lived in Shechem; had two

reunite in communion with Our Lord Jesus Christ, the Word of God on Earth.

Yet Joseph, a man strict in his ways, discovering his betrothed with the early signs of pregnancy—knowing he had not known her as a wife—turned to his God, and with a pained heart, cast a look of pity on his fiancée, thinking to spare her shame by fleeing from her side, seeking in the absence of his love the consolation that religion might offer him in his sorrows.

No sooner had that thought entered Joseph's mind than the angel of the Lord took his place beside him, revealing to him the whole truth regarding the Most Holy Virgin.

Joseph, a humble Spirit, a soul devoted to the Lord's service, accepted his apparent fatherhood of Our Lord Jesus Christ, regarding the Holy Virgin forever as the spouse of God.

Jesus was then upon Earth; the sacrifice prepared by the Eternal's own hand was ready to receive the Lamb without blemish, who would redeem men from sin.

How He would develop His doctrine, how He was understood, loved, and rejected by men, how He laid the foundations of the Christian Church, now so distorted, how He filled the apostles' souls with flames of faith, hope, and love, sending them to preach His Good News everywhere, and how He will return among men to receive the fruits of their labors—this is what we shall attempt to convey, imploring the mercy of God, the light of Our Lord Jesus Christ, and the assistance of His apostles.

---

golden calves cast in Bethel and Dan, whose worship he commanded. He sacrificed to these false gods, when the prophet Jadon foretold the downfall of his cult and the death of his priests. Furious, Jeroboam stretched out his hand to silence him, but it immediately withered, and he only recovered from that evil through the prophet's prayers. He died, leaving the throne to Nadab, his son.

CHAPTER II

Birth of the Divine Master. — Hymns heard by the shepherds. — Moses crosses the Red Sea. — The golden calf. — Moses orders the great hecatomb.

Serving more the interests of a dynasty that became renowned for the oppression it exercised over a humble and weak people than the Hebrew national will—already manifested by all its branches—Caesar Augustus, the Roman emperor, chose, of his own accord, to divide the Kingdom of Judea into three principalities, under the direct rule of the descendants of Herod, called the Great, notorious for the ferocity of his crimes committed against the Divine Code.

Princes of Judea, Archelaus, Philip, and Antipas could well continue the legacy of their ancestor by massacring the Jewish people, for they had a carte blanche from Caesar, who, shielded by the might of his conquering armies, would never allow the humble people to raise their heads, not even to claim the right to have a religion.

The dawn of redemption was already adorning the horizons of Palestine with the most resplendent colors; yet the despots of the Earth, blinded by vanity and ambition and entrenched in their pride, were hurling their final darts at the image of freedom embodied in the Son of Mary, in the son of the humble carpenter—Jesus, Our Lord.

And, just as the soldiers tore the Nazarene's tunic at the foot of the cross, competing for the largest share, so Caesar, wishing to have the greatest number of subservient subjects—slaves—under his control, ordered a vast census throughout his domains to determine the exact number of the people over whom he exercised his rule, according to his will.

Obeying this edict, Joseph and the Most Holy Virgin, Galileans that they were, went to the city of Bethlehem, where the divine union of God with His creatures was to be consummated.

But precisely because the people were called en masse to register, and because the city was small, Joseph and Mary did not find accommodations at the inn or in the home of friends to shelter them; every place was taken and the two holy travelers were compelled to take refuge in the rough shelter of a simple stable to escape the inclement weather.

And thus man, believing he could subjugate a free people under his will, paved the way for the fulfillment of the prophecies, causing the Most Holy Virgin to seek out Bethlehem to give birth, according to the belief of those peoples, to the Child God—the Savior of Israel.

Our Lord Jesus Christ begins, at His very birth, by giving the world the most extraordinary example of humility. He starts by provoking a great scandal in Judea, choosing for His appearance on Earth a humble shelter, while the Jewish people, ever taking the words of the prophets literally, believed that the promised Messiah would be one of the greatest kings on Earth, ruling Judea materially and establishing a kingdom so vast and so immense as to absorb all other realms and empires.

And so it could have been!

The Divine Redeemer could have chosen the grand gilded palaces and all the pomp and splendor of the Earth for His appearance; He had the power to do so. But it was fitting that people should receive His first example of humility at the very moment of His entrance into the world; it was necessary to show human vanity how a grain of sand can absorb a mountain, how a drop of water can contain an ocean.

Away from the Virgin, looking for provisions in the Bethlehem market, Joseph went to buy food for himself and his companion.

Enraptured, saturated with divine fluids, the Immaculate Virgin found herself in that holy trance that only pure Spirits can enjoy; when she emerged from her profound rapture, she heard, out in the fields where the little lambs were bleating, sonorous hymns rising through the skies, giving glory to God in the highest and peace to men on Earth. Filled with confusion and reverence before her unimaginable fruit, she found her Child God in her arms.

The first smiles between Heaven and Earth were exchanged; God Himself, in the person of Our Lord Jesus Christ, was transfused into the human soul. And the shepherds, who kept watch by night, asked among themselves: What has happened in Israel? Whose are these songs that fill the silent night?

And the holy Spirits, producing the luminous and sonorous fluids, said to the innocent souls of the shepherds: The King of Judea is born, the Christ, Our Lord, so long awaited!

Yes, luminous and sonic fluids were the hymns produced by the heavenly host—this same fluid formed by the will of the Spirits appointed to the mission of Our Lord Jesus Christ, and which was seen as the semblance of a great star, guiding the Magi to the lands of Bethlehem.

That same fluid, immeasurably luminous, formed the pillar of fire in the rugged foreign lands, opening a path for the captives of Egypt across the waters of the Red Sea—an extraordinary event that, in the eyes of the wise, is nothing but a legend produced by the imagination of Eastern peoples, for they have, to this day, failed to understand the laws that governed that extraordinary phenomenon.

The Red Sea, so called because of the presence of microscopic algae, which science today knows under the name protococcus, giving its waters their characteristic color—despite scholarly contradictions—did indeed grant free passage to the Jewish people, led by the great lawgiver Moses, on their way to the lands of Canaan.

I will dwell on this biblical point because I wish my brothers on Earth to understand the great slaughter of which I will speak shortly—the slaughter of the innocent.

Moses, an enlightened Spirit, a medium gifted with all forms of mediumship, assisted by the celestial elite on account of the high mission he carried out on Earth, knew the flow and ebb of the Red Sea perfectly well.

He tried, through supplication more than once, to obtain freedom for his people; through invoking plagues, he sought to quell those hatreds harbored against his race, subjugated to the most thankless form of servitude.

The king was unmoved by Moses's pleas, unafraid of the wrath of the Lord, manifested through various phenomena that human language has termed plagues. Moses then asked the king, the lord of his people, at the very least to permit him and his people to go three days' journey to fulfill a promise they had made to their God.

As what we on Earth call the equinoctial tides approached—the planetary movement that produces the sea's ebb and flow—the Spirit of the king was touched so that he consented to Moses and the Hebrew people fulfilling their promise. And so, with the great Jewish throng and their flocks, Moses set out on the road to Canaan, crossing precisely at the hour designated by the higher Spirits, through the strait where the great ebb of the waters took place.

But pay close attention: only a long time after Moses and his people had departed did the king, informed by his advisers and effectively emerging from that stupor induced by the higher Spirits, order his legions to pursue the Jews, exactly at the moment of the waters' flow, which hindered their passage. This was something they could not fathom and was known only to the medium, the prophet Moses, through the intuition he received from the high Spirits of the Lord.

Avoiding passage through various kingdoms whose politics and religion differed from those of the Hebrew people, Moses entered the desert. Reaching a broad plain that lines the foothills of Mount Sinai, he commanded them to set up tents and wait for him while he went to speak with the Lord of Hosts, with the Lord God of Israel.

The hardships endured by the liberated people in the desert led them more than once to bitter complaints against their liberator; more than once, they rebelled against Moses, asking him to lead them back to the land of captivity, for that had been preferable to dying of hunger, thirst, or being devoured by wild beasts.

Moses climbed Mount Sinai to establish communication with Melchizedek, the King of Salem[5], namely, Our Lord Jesus Christ, since Melchizedek is merely a name used by our Divine Master when appearing tangibly to Abraham and also to Moses.

The people, however, grew impatient waiting for the prophet's return; the sermons of their liberator, his teachings—these signified some truth to them, but they lacked the essential element: an image of God, the object of their worship. And thus, in that desperation of belief, in that feverish idolatry, they forced Aaron to make a god for them, similar to that of the gentiles, for their devotions.

Aaron[6], terrified before thousands of men, women, and children clamoring for a symbol, ordered everyone to contribute their jewelry for the creation of their deity. Digging into the ground, he crudely cast, according to the techniques of those times, the golden calf.

They were in the midst of merrymaking, chanting songs—not the Passover hymns, but the songs learned in Egypt. Gathered around their symbol of the god, they reveled joyfully, committing the most abhorrent of all crimes!

---

[5] Salem: the ancient name of Jerusalem.
[6] Moses's older brother, from the tribe of Levi, born in Egypt; he assisted Moses in liberating the Hebrew people from Pharaoh's yoke.

Moses descended the mountain bearing the tablets of the law. Hearing their music, he questioned Melchizedek, who intuitively explained what was happening.

Then the prophet, the inspired man, vanished, and Moses the man appeared before the people, wounded in his spirit—in what he held most pure and sacred: the love of the one true God! He confronted Aaron, demanding explanations. Aaron tried to justify his actions, but Moses, overpowering him with his authority, made him, so to speak, his adjutant, and commanded him to go among all the tents with the sons of Levi—the only ones who had not worshipped the golden calf—and carry out the great slaughter.

Having thus explained, in rough words, what you can better read and understand in Exodus, Chapter XXXII, let us now return to Palestine, where we will meet our Divine Master in the temple, among the doctors.

CHAPTER III

Easter celebrations. — Jesus among the doctors. — Baptism of Jesus. — Confession. — Imprisonment and death of the Precursor. — Beheading of the innocents. — Original sin. — John the Baptist, reincarnation of Elijah. — Temptation of the Divine Master in the desert by the devil.

Following the laws and customs of their forebears, the virtuous man Joseph, accompanied by the Spouse of God, attended the Easter celebrations instituted by the great legislator Moses to commemorate the day on which the Hebrew people went from the lands of captivity to the lands promised to their freedom.

Obeying, likewise, the needs of a series of events that were about to take place in the settings of Palestine, Jesus, accompanied by his cousin-brothers, in the apparent form of a twelve-year-old boy, also attended those same celebrations. Once the seven days devoted to them had passed, he left his relatives and friends and went into the great synagogue to debate with the doctors of the law, that is, the men chosen among the most competent to preach to the people the Mosaic laws, the prophecies, and all those masterpieces of the Old Testament which later formed the Canon of the Church, through the efforts of Ezra[7] and Nehemiah[8] on behalf of the Jewish people, who, being divided and without religious guidance, had then given themselves over to the most absurd practices of idolatry, publicly airing the most extravagant ideas imaginable when compared with the teachings bestowed by the prophets.

Jesus among the doctors!

But where had that twelve-year-old child, without teachers, books, or schools, drawn all that knowledge which astonished the most competent, the elder priests of the law?

How could that boy, by flashes of eloquence, confound those who deemed themselves masters of all religious sciences—he, the humble son of the carpenter, whose intelligence, in the opinion of those who heard him, could not possibly possess the wisdom he was displaying?

This is the fact that, in those times, caused astonishment among the doctors of the law, and that still amazes those today who do not seek to study the Gospel in spirit and in truth!

With us, however, it does not awaken the same sentiment, since, by the revelation that we have received through God's mercy, we know that within that seemingly small child's body was incarnated, in all its might, the wisdom of the Creator; and thus, that child was the Word of God, apparently humanized.

Jesus—says the evangelist Luke in Chapter II, verse 52—was growing in stature and in wisdom before God and men.

But we ask: Was Jesus truly growing in age, wisdom, and grace, as the evangelist states?

Is this passage of the Gospel itself a revelation, an inference from the evangelist Luke, or merely the judgment of man?

Could Jesus, a supremely elevated and pure Spirit, remain permanently imprisoned in his body, even though a heavenly one, on the surface of the Earth, growing day by day in the presence of men?

Certainly not.

---

[7] Jewish doctor who lived in the 5th century before Christ. He obtained from Artaxerxes, king of the Persians, permission to bring the Jews back to their fathers and rebuild the temple of Jerusalem. Having arrived in that city, Ezra reestablished worship services, gathered together the canonical books, and explained them skillfully, which earned him the title "prince of the doctors of the law."

[8] A Jew, born in Babylon, who rebuilt the walls of Jerusalem despite the opposition of the enemies of his nation. He governed the Jewish people with great wisdom. He aided Ezra in coordinating the books and completing the Canon.

And, if we study the Holy Scriptures with full discernment, we arrive at the conclusion that the Divine Master, through his own words, declared he did not have a permanent life on Earth. He did, however, make himself visible to his relatives and friends whenever he deemed it necessary.

— I leave life in order to take it up again, he said more than once, and if we seek the spirit of that phrase, we will interpret it thus: I leave this body whenever I desire, to resume the tasks of my heavenly governance.

Hence we find, in the Bible, the Divine Nazarene in the straw of a manger and then see him again only at twelve years of age. From that point until he was thirty, a mysterious veil seems to obscure his identity, until we find him on the way to the Jordan to seek John, from whom he was to receive the waters of baptism.

And the relatives and friends of the Divine Master, whenever they saw him raising paralytics and performing acts of the most astonishing wonder, would exclaim, so says the Gospel: Is this not the son of Joseph and Mary?

They did so because, upon passing more than once by the humble hut of the carpenter, those who were clairvoyant mediums would see there the young Nazarene smiling at the arduous work of the one considered his father.

And Joseph and Mary, themselves mediums, whenever they called him in thought on the most pure rays of their love, would find their Blessed Son in the realms of light; and he was always present in the home of his family, through the hearts and souls of the good.

Thus do we understand the greatness of the Lord; thus do we conceive the possibility that he was present to his family and to the friends of his household whenever it was needed.

Moreover, the fact that the Virgin Mary, our Most Holy Mother, noticing the absence of the Divine Master when returning from the Easter celebrations, shows us that he was not always with them; for we cannot imagine that loving and devoted parents, even without the noble qualities of soul that the man Joseph and the Blessed Virgin possessed, would wait three whole days before missing, in the ordinary sense, the fruit of their blessed love.

Yet Jesus did require that rebuke from the Virgin—if rebuke we may call those outbursts of love. He needed, let us say, the laments of the Most Holy Virgin in order to teach men, through example from the very start, that they must leave father, mother, siblings, and friends to attend, according to his own words, the things of God, the affairs of his Father.

Yes, he said it: He who does not leave father, mother, and friends for my sake, for God's sake, is not worthy of being my disciple! It is a wise and grand teaching that instructs mankind to abandon all worldly attachments and personal interests for the service of their Creator and Father alone, to whom they owe all mercies and all favors of the purest and truest love!

In the Gospel of Luke, Chapter III, verses 21 and 22, we find Our Lord Jesus Christ receiving the waters of baptism before the multitude surrounding the beloved son of Elizabeth and Zacharias.

The evangelist says that once Jesus had been baptized, heaven opened, and the Holy Spirit, in the form of a dove, descended upon him, and a voice was heard saying: You are that specially beloved Son of mine; in you is all my delight!

Heaven opened! No; the space was illuminated, adorned with the most resplendent fluids that lend beauty to pure Spirits, and these declared: This is the beloved Son, in whom the Lord has placed all his delight!

We cannot conceive that heaven literally opened and that the Creator, in the form of a dove, descended to tell Our Lord Jesus Christ the words that were heard. Rather, we believe that, at the moment when the Divine Jesus embarked upon his great mission on Earth by receiving the waters of baptism from his precursor, the phalanx of good Spirits—of holy Spirits that accompanied him from the beyond on his grand endeavor—revealed itself to the clairvoyant mediums, proclaiming publicly to the crowd that he was the beloved Son in whom the Lord had placed all his delight.

And John, in the presence of the one whose sandal straps he deemed himself unfit to untie, testified about him, saying: This is the one of whom I said that he would come after me and that he was preferred over me, for he was before me.

— Repent, he went on, do penance, for the axe is already in his hands, and every tree that does not bear good fruit shall be cut down; publicly confess your crimes, cleanse your consciences and souls, so that you may receive the light that comes from above; decorate your homes, the dwellings of your Spirits, in order to welcome the Chosen One!

And thus proceeded the precursor of Our Lord Jesus Christ! And thus must continue all those who today possess a perfect understanding of the evangelical teachings!

We understand public confession, that is, the demonstrations of humility of the Spirit who confesses before God and his brothers, promising not to commit the same offenses again. And with apologies to the present-day Church:

More prudent than its priests—who call themselves Christ's representatives on Earth and ministers of God—were the priests of Buddha[9] back when, in India's public squares, not to hear the people's confessions in secret but to reveal their own failings and weaknesses, they would summon everyone, asking for help in the mission that weighed upon them to spread the ideas of the founders of their religious sect.

And those priests, by the way, practiced chastity, covering themselves in the rags gathered from the trash heaps; whatever they received from the people was spent for the good of those same people, never for their own benefit.

Forgive us, Church, if, on this point as well, we do not see you aligned with the teachings of Our Lord Jesus Christ.

The teaching of the apostles states clearly: I, a sinner, confess to Almighty God; it does not say: I confess to man, as much a sinner or even more of a sinner than I. And though censure and excommunication may fall upon this book, permit the voice from the tomb to declare plainly: the current confession practiced by the Church is a crime before God!

John the Baptist, making no distinctions of person, denounced the misconduct of both small and great. He went so far as to censure the incestuous acts committed by Herod with Herodias, the wife of one of his brothers.

The great ruler, regarding John's censure as an affront to his high dignity as governor of Judea and swayed by the requests and pleas of Herodias—who considered herself wronged in her dreams of being an honest wife while living with a man who was not her husband, and to further fill the cup of his misdeeds—ordered the imprisonment of the gentle son of Elizabeth. His order was carried out, and in prison, extending his loving thoughts to the home of his parents and

---

[9] A name in the Buddhist religion that represents perfect reason, absolute intelligence. This name also applies to the various incarnations of the supreme reason, the principal of which is Cakyamuni or Siddhartha Gautama, a wise man of India, the son of the Prince of Bahar, of the royal Cakya lineage. At the age of 29, Cakyamuni withdrew into the desert and, gaining perfect knowledge, was considered Buddha. He made a great number of disciples, ascended a tree, and there died after two and a half months of meditation.

connecting himself in spirit to Our Lord Jesus Christ, who visited him constantly, John, full of holy resignation, awaited the hour of his release, the atonement for the sins committed by Moses and Elijah.

He awaited, in the silence of his prison, the day of the Judean king's birthday in order to present him not with gold or with the precious Eastern gems that are the lofty adornments of the mighty, but with his own head—with a part of his body that would stand, in the annals of history, as the great testimony of his repentance when, departing the existences of Moses and Elijah, he had come, in spirit, to understand that none may violate God's laws, or break his commandments that place, above all else, love of God himself and of one's neighbor, even if done in defense of the most just and sacred causes.

Amid the splendor of the celebration in his palace, peopled by the highest dignitaries according to society's standards, Herod, at Herodias's request and after swearing the most dreadful oath, interrupted, for an instant, the festivities. He summoned the captain of his guard and ordered the head of the Baptist brought to him, the audacious prophet who had dared—forgetting that he was dealing with the greatest of all men in Judea—to rebuke him openly in the public square!

Silence fell; the instruments were stilled for a few moments, and Herod's servant left the palace for the prison where the virtuous captive lay, to carry out the king's command by severing his beautiful, fair head.

But first Jesus, the divine friend, the compassionate Jesus, had entered that prison and, like a dove of hope in the tempestuous sea of those disordered passions, had brought, like an olive branch to Elizabeth's son, the sublime pardon for the offenses he had committed when, a wanderer on Earth, he bore the name Moses, when, a pilgrim on Earth, he was called Elijah!

And John, receiving the pardon of the Divine Master within the fortress in which Herod was holding him prisoner, was seized by the most extraordinary courage and, undaunted, awaited the arrival of the soldier who would execute that peremptory order!

In spirit, he returned to times past, recalling the acts of cruelty he had committed when, as Moses, he rebuked the people for raising up the golden calf to worship; and recalling the days of Elijah, when, on Mount Carmel, as a fervent believer, he had the prophets of Baal put to the sword. Thus John offered thanks to Our Lord Jesus Christ for allowing him to redeem, in the person of the Precursor, all the sins of his past while also carrying out the great mission of preparing the

Lord's path and being the voice that cries in the wilderness, summoning the people to repentance and atonement!

And, remembering the past, he still offered thanks to the Lord for having descended to Earth accompanied by the children of Levi's tribe, the so-called innocents, who likewise had to bear their heads, as part of the most extraordinary cortege for the coming of the Chosen One!

And only thus can we understand the justice of God, which acts equally upon the least of creatures and upon the Precursor of Our Lord Jesus Christ.

Beheading of the innocents!

But now, we who know the Gospel in spirit and truth—now that original sin, which according to the Church comes to us from our forebears, is a dead letter in our consciousness and understanding—now that we more fully comprehend the greatness, justice, and mercy of God, we cannot admit that innocents, as the evangelists literally have it and as the world imagines them, could suffer such barbarity at the hands of Herod if they had not, at some point, committed crimes worthy of such punishment!

No; the crimes had indeed been committed—we can see that already in the passage I referred to in another chapter, concerning the golden calf, and also in the Third Book of Kings, Chapter XVIII, when Elijah needed to give idolaters a sign that his God was the one true God.

Yet some will say: How can you prove that John the Baptist was the reincarnation of Elijah?

I prove nothing, I reply to those who read me. The Gospel proves everything for me, and it is to the Gospel that I confine myself in my argument.

Thus, when the Angel of the Lord announced Elizabeth's conception, the evangelist tells us that the Precursor would appear in the spirit and power of Elijah[10]. When the people asked the Divine Master about Elijah's promised coming, he told them that Elijah had already come, yet they did not recognize him[11].

Moreover, the fact that the Jews expected Elijah's return—an expectation resting on Elisha's account, in which he claims his master had been taken up into the heavens by lightning, for being clairvoyant he saw the prophet's perispirit ascending on high—forms a cluster of truths that today are explained by the revelation of revelations, the

---

[10] Luke, Chapter I, verse 17.
[11] Matthew, Chapter XVII, verses 12 and 13. Mark, Chapter IX, verse 13.

Spiritism that we study.

Elijah had to return, so the Jews believed, and he did indeed return in the person of John the Baptist, not only to prepare the Lord's path but to endure the trial for sins committed in other lifetimes. And yet, a pilgrim of love like Our Lord Jesus Christ, he was on Earth the most exalted Spirit among men born of women[12].

But referring to the Divine Nazarene, John said to those who had been sent to him to ask who he was[13]: I am not worthy to untie the straps of his sandals; I baptize men in the waters of the Jordan; the Divine Master baptizes them with fire and the Holy Spirit!

See there, reader, a terrible dilemma from which reason cannot escape: either Our Lord Jesus Christ did not tell the truth—which is impossible—or else John really was the greatest among those born of women, and that would mean that Jesus was not counted among them because he was over the Earth, or else—and this is the truth—Jesus was not the son of any woman, being solely and entirely the Son of God, presented to the world in the outward form of a man like ourselves, with his perispirit passing through the womb of a Pure and Immaculate Virgin!

That, it seems to me, is the truth, as also it seems true that the temptation of Jesus in the desert by Satan, as found in the Gospels[14], was impossible.

The temptation of Jesus!

But for there to be temptation, there must be susceptibility to sin; where there is susceptibility to sin, there is no purity—and Jesus was pure, as we know!

Could that temptation mentioned in the Gospel be an inference, a deduction made by the evangelist himself?

If Jesus was tempted by the devil in the desert, who in that desert heard the voice of temptation and the responses of the Righteous One?

Or could it have been a revelation?

We do not think so, and it seems it was merely a supposition on the part of the evangelists. It was customary for all prophets to seek the desert before beginning their missions, to prepare themselves—through prayer and penance—for the tasks and works of their faith.

And, once John had declared him the Lamb of God, the Savior of Israel, the Jewish people at once wanted to proclaim him their absolute king, the highest position they believed they could offer him. The

---

[12] Matthew, Chapter XI, verse 11. Luke, Chapter VII, verse 28.
[13] John, Chapter I, verses 19 to 27.
[14] Matthew, Chapter IV, verses 1 to 11. Luke, Chapter IV, verses 1 to 13.

Divine Master, however, who saw into all hearts and perceived that such a display of will was influenced by hidden forces seeking to divert him from fulfilling his holy mission, began preaching to the people about temptation. From this fact, his disciples concluded that he had been tempted in the desert by the devil, because he had begun preparing them in his sermons on temptation, so that they might overcome it.

Furthermore, in the same Gospel, we see that inferior Spirits, from a great distance, could not withstand the presence of Jesus, shouting: What have we to do with you, Jesus the Nazarene?[15] If the mere presence of the Divine Master drove away evil Spirits, bringing peace and calm to the wretchedly obsessed, how can we imagine that Satan—if Satan existed—could have spoken face to face with Our Lord Jesus Christ, offering him the glories of Earth?

It would be like imagining darkness dimming the brilliance of the sun, trying to draw from the density of its own shadows a light capable of outshining the great star!

Satan is ourselves; Satan is any who do not do the will of God and do not follow the doctrine of Our Lord Jesus Christ.

Satan is our pride, our vanity, our greed; it is all our perverse instincts that place us on a dreadful mountain of temptations, luring us toward the abyss, where we should find the shadows of an eternal death if our soul's hardness were eternal—if our wicked impulses were everlasting.

Satan!

So did God create Satan?! Did Good, in its purest form, draw from itself a particle and create this imaginary being, endowing him with such power to tempt that even Christ could be tempted?!

And are we then unable to withstand or to escape his influence, for he has nearly as great a power for evil as God does for good?!

No; in evil itself we find the supreme revelation of God's love and mercy.

Meditating on Creation, we discover nothing more beautiful and exalted than free will, our freedom. From it stems our capacity to become gods, as Our Lord Jesus Christ said[16].

From it arises the greatness of our own merit, the exaltation of our Spirits, particles of the Creator, seeking of their own endeavor, in perfect freedom, to unite with the Great Whole. That is sublime; that

---

[15] Mark, Chapter I, verses 23 to 27. Also Chapter III, verses 11 and 12. Luke, Chapter IV, verses 33 to 37.

[16] John, Chapter X, verses 22 to 36.

is of God. But Satan, the angel of darkness, supposedly created *ad aeterno*, according to the Church, to tempt man, is nothing but an absurdity.

With this understanding, as Christians in Christ, we must search day by day, hour by hour, moment by moment, for that terrible figure that frightens us, hidden in the shadow of our conscience. There, in our hearts, in the recesses of our souls, we must find that being that can condemn us to hell through hatred, through pride, through all those pernicious feelings that form the demon's retinue.

Whoever loves, who knows how to love the Lord his God above all things and his neighbor as himself—whoever has charity, compassion, the capacity to walk the shining path of the Nazarene, sharing his affections among his brothers—whoever has faith and truly believes and hopes in the promises of Our Lord Jesus Christ—such a person may proudly say, as a true Christian: I am free from the devil; my house is swept and adorned; I can receive the visit of my Guide without trembling; I can receive the visit of Our Lord Jesus Christ, my Divine Master, with head unbowed!

Christians in Christ, have love, have charity, have faith, and declare with a loud voice to the Church: Away, away with that dreadful shadow of the devil! Within me there exist the virtues that I received, as seeds, from the Creator and that have sprouted under the breath of the Divine Master. They have grown and now their flowers have bloomed, and from their fragrance arises the true incense that purifies me in this church of flesh, where my spirit confesses and prays to its true God!

CHAPTER IV

Wedding at Cana. — Jesus expels the merchants from the temple. — The fair of the sacraments. — Spiritism is the forerunner of the Spirit of Truth. — Nicodemus's question to the Divine Master. — The law of reincarnation. — Hell. — The tenants of the Lord's Vineyard. — The resurrection of the Spirit. — Jesus and the Samaritan woman[17].

Terrified by Herod's dreadful act, John's disciples seek solace for their sorrows in the gentle and loving bosom of Our Lord Jesus Christ; they join the Lord's disciples and, with them, try to fill that tremendous void left in their souls by the disappearance of their most beloved Master.

Jesus welcomes them into His loving bosom, consoles their afflicted hearts, and benevolently allows these humble ones whom He has chosen for His bitter yet sweet task to become part of the communion of His disciples.

Along with Jesus's family, they go to attend the wedding at Cana, the sublime pretext by which the Divine Master begins what are called miracles, once again showing humanity that He was not the son of a woman.

Seated on His mat, having chosen the last place at the table, Jesus has at His side the Most Holy Virgin, as well as His cousin-brothers, the sons of Mary Cleophas, who were also invited to the wedding.

The evangelist tells us that, the feast being almost over, Jesus's mother, noticing that the amphoras were empty, turned to Her beloved Son and, in a gentle phrase of lament, said to Him: They have no more

---

[17] John, Chapter II.

wine; to which the Lord replied: Woman, what is that to Me and to you; what do we have in common with this?

The Virgin turns to the servants and says: Do everything He tells you.

Present in the banquet hall were several jars used for the purifications customary among the Jews; the Lord ordered that they be filled with water, and once His mandate was fulfilled, everyone was served the most delicious nectar one can imagine, which caused the headwaiter to address the bridegroom, asking why he had saved the best wine for the end of the banquet, having served the poorer wine first.

We, however, who do not see that event in the same light, will say that the Divine Master, possessing great power over the fluids involved in the economy of life—mineral, vegetable, and animal alike—imposed upon the water the color of wine and its taste on the palate of those whom He had magnetized by His presence at the wedding in Cana.

Therefore, never back then, just as it cannot happen today, nor shall it ever happen, have there been miracles if, as the orthodox would have it, that word means a derogation of natural laws.

Jesus thus imbued those jars, by His mere will, with the necessary fluids to fulfill the wish of the Virgin Mary and, at the same time, begin His great mission.

At the end of the banquet, the evangelist tells us, the Divine Master heads to Capernaum, but as the Passover feast draws near, He remains there only a short while before proceeding with His entire entourage to the city of Jerusalem.

Upon arriving, He enters the temple and finds it turned into a place of the most shameful traffic; then, consumed by zeal, He takes up some cords and expels the merchants, declaring that His Father's house is a house of prayer and not a den of thieves[18].

But we ask, could it be possible that Jesus, gentleness personified, the most extraordinary love ever to descend to Earth—Jesus, the compassionate, the merciful—would take a scourge and, in a fit of rage, physically punish His brothers, even had He been consumed by zeal for His Father's house?

Certainly not.

Place in the Divine Master's hands a lash of light; imagine Him revealing Himself in all His grandeur before the temple's profaners;

---

[18] Matthew, Chapter XXI, verse 13. Mark, Chapter XI, verse 17. Luke, Chapter XIX, verse 46.

envision the mob of merchants collapsing to the ground, astonished and confused, in the face of the great light emanating from the Divine Nazarene, and thus you will behold the scourge that Jesus used!

And despite that entirely moral chastisement, and in spite of all His teachings, which have endured for centuries, the fair of Jerusalem sets up its stalls inside the Church in the most ignominious fashion, causing the deepest sorrow for truly Christian spirits, because if, in former times, people sold birds and meek lambs intended for burnt offerings, today the fair of the sacraments is held!

Oh! Allow me to speak the whole truth, for if Jesus does not come down to Earth once again to expel the merchants from the temple, nevertheless He allows His workers—even the humblest of His disciples—to lift the slab from the tomb and show Christendom His divine and most sacred image, which certainly is not the one you present in your pompous cathedrals!

Nor can the tinsel or the splendor of your temples ever stifle, within your reliquaries, the voice of your own conscience, which cries out to you, in the name of Jesus, in the name of Peter, the founder of the Church, that what you do today is no more and no less than what your ancestors—slaves to idolatry—did in the temples of Jerusalem!

What? He whom you profess to represent on Earth—He who, less favored than the wild beasts in their hidden caves, had nowhere to lay His head[19]—Jesus, the wanderer of love who strove everywhere to wipe the tears of the afflicted, pouring into their sorrowful hearts the balm of His immeasurable love—do you say that this is the one you deny bringing to the bedsides of the sick and dying, symbolically in the viaticum, except in exchange for a vile coin?

Jesus, who entered Levi's home to share in the publican's banquet and who, when censured for doing so, said that He had come into the world for the sick[20], He who always gave preference to the unfortunate—does He now refuse symbolically to ascend, in the form of a host wafting in clouds of incense in the priest's hands, in supplication for those who lacked sufficient courage to fight life's battles?

Jesus, who recommended that the repentant should pray far from the public square so as not to resemble the scribes and Pharisees who

---

[19] Matthew, Chapter VIII, verses 19 and 20. Luke, Chapter IX, verses 57 and 58.
[20] Matthew, Chapter IX, verses 9 to 13. Mark, Chapter II, verses 14 to 17. Luke, Chapter V, verses 27 to 32.

made a great show of crying out their beliefs[21], does He now enter the confessional to, yet again in exchange for vile money, pardon humanity's sins?

He, who always opposed the will of the Jewish people, who wished to proclaim Him king, could He possibly incline the priests toward a theocratic rule?

Certainly not! That is not the Jesus we wish to present to Christendom in our humble work.

And despite the lash of our words, we lament that you, priests, bear upon your shoulders the most terrible of responsibilities—the accountability of conscience before God, the accountability of your calling, which you yourselves requested, not for the commerce of Jerusalem, not for the commerce of sacraments, but for the uplifting of the Christian soul until it meets its Divine Shepherd up in those realms of light, where dwell the elect, the true Christians!

Forgive me if I speak to you thus; but we, too, bear responsibilities: we have great commitments that remain unsettled. And before the harvest arrives—before the Spirit of Truth comes to separate the wheat from the chaff, rendering to each according to their works—allow the children of the tomb, allow the living to come speak to the dead, waking them from that lethargy of passions that has blinded so many spirits, to the point that on Earth's surface one rarely finds that path of light which, so many centuries ago, was trodden by the Divine Lamb, attracting, like a sun of love, the souls entrusted to Him by the Eternal, for their salvation and happiness.

Allow the living to come forth from the tombs to say to all of you: Christians in Christ, take up the Gospel; meditate upon these truths; do penance, for Spiritism is the forerunner of the Spirit of Truth!

It is the Consoler promised by Our Lord Jesus Christ to His disciples, as well as to all humankind, to ease pain, lessen sorrows, and alleviate afflictions in the hours of tribulation and great suffering!

Behold it among you, manifesting itself day by day across the Earth, like the voice of John crying out, calling the people to the new baptism of the Holy Spirit—to penance and repentance. And as once the scribes and Pharisees, the doctors of the law, restraining their spite and hatred, approached the Beloved Lamb, asking Him by what authority He broke with the customs of the time and with the laws established by themselves, the Church's leaders—so, too, will you today demand wonders, great miracles, so that you might discover by what authority

---

[21] Matthew, Chapter VI, verses 5 to 8.

we interrupt the progress of your ecclesiastical affairs, disturbing the apparent serenity of your consciences with the word from the tomb.

To the scribes and Pharisees, the doctors of the law, Jesus replied: Destroy this temple, and in three days I will raise it up—referring, as the evangelist makes clear, to the temple of His body which, coveted by hatred, would later fall, only to rise again; to modern doctors of the law, to the new scribes and Pharisees, the promised Consoler—that is, the commissioned Spirits in service to the Beloved Master's vineyard—might reply: Destroy the truth, if you can, and only then will Spiritism vanish from the face of the Earth; convene new councils and ordain therein the disappearance of truth, and from the lips of the tombs, like the stones on the road to Jerusalem[22], will ring out the voices of the Lord's messengers, proclaiming everywhere the observance of the true Gospel, the fulfillment of the Crucified One's Doctrine, so poorly understood and so greatly cheapened by your ambitions!

We do our duty; we do not wish to hide under a bushel the light that the Almighty has mercifully bestowed on us.

From atop the rooftops of your own houses we shall cry out for the truth and only the truth that we have learned. And, as a humble plant, perhaps sprouting in stony ground amid thorns, thriving under the dews of divine mercy, we strive, within the limitations of our earthly bounds, to grow and bear fruit, testifying that we have received in the corolla of our soul the holy and sacred dew that descends to us through the love of Our Lord Jesus Christ.

Acting so, we fulfill our duty; let the Church fulfill hers, but let her do so with a truly Christian conscience!

After refusing to perform marvels for the scribes and Pharisees who requested them in order to bear witness to Him—as if the Divine Master needed any witness other than His own—Jesus departed Jerusalem for Judea, where He was sought by one of Israel's teachers, named Nicodemus[23]. Ashamed and dreading the censure of the people should they learn that he was seeking to hear the son of a humble carpenter on religious matters, Nicodemus waited for nightfall, as though he were a great criminal, to approach the Divine Lamb.

Greeting the Divine Master, Nicodemus—who sensed that Jesus was a great Spirit sent to Earth, as His deeds testified to His spiritual rank—confesses this insight, asking what he must do to be saved.

Jesus seizes the opportunity afforded Him and replies to the elder

---

[22] Luke, Chapter XIX, verse 40.
[23] John, Chapter III, verses 1 to 12.

priest, saying, under the veil of words, that no Spirit descended to Earth can enter the Kingdom of God without being born again of water and the Holy Spirit.

The word water, used by the Divine Master, conveys two meanings, one suited to the scientific knowledge of that time, and another that still applies today to all those who do not know the truth according to the doctrine of salvation.

Thus, among the Jews, water was regarded as the generative principle of all things, the original element from which everything in the organic realms was derived; and so it was a dogma for them, whose basis we find in Moses's Genesis[24].

Now, if water was the foundational element of all material things, it would, by implication, generate the new bodies needed by the Spirits who, once condemned to suffer for straying from the path of light, required those bodies so that, by progressing and purifying themselves, they might enter God's Kingdom, merging into that pure, luminous existence that is the Spirit's true life.

However, as we said, this word also expressed another concept: the new birth by the waters of baptism, that is, by repentance and the conversion of souls to the domains of truth and the Holy Spirit, until they reach the relative perfection to which we are all called, so that we might know God in the fullness of His grace and infinite love.

Nicodemus, steeped in his ancestors' prejudices, despite being a teacher in Israel, believed Jesus referred to resurrection—that is, to the Spirit's reentry into the same body—another dogma among the Jews. Thus they believed that the prophets returned again to Earth, which is why they awaited the return of Elijah, as shown in the Gospels: Mark, Chapter VIII, Luke, Chapter IX, and Matthew, Chapter XVI.

Jesus, however, surprised by Nicodemus's ignorance—he was, after all, a teacher in Israel, yet had not understood His words—tells him plainly: You must be born again.

In light of this categorical assertion by the Divine Master, we should ask those who study sacred matters in good faith whether the words of Our Lord Jesus Christ can in any way be explained without reconciling them with the reincarnation of Spirits?

Is there any argument capable of proving that, by telling Nicodemus that he must be born again, Jesus was referring to baptism alone? Certainly not.

---

[24] Genesis, Chapter I, verses 2, 6, 7, 9, 10, 20 and Chapter II, verses 1, 4, 5, 6, 7.

Jesus affirmed the natural law of the reincarnation of Spirits; and in this law—which expresses all the love of our Creator and Father—creatures, even those who the Church condemns to the undying flames of hell, find their salvation. In this sublime law of justice and love, the repentant Spirit finds the means of regeneration and happiness; it is through it that the fallen angels on Earth return to heaven, making use of Jacob's symbolic ladder—the grace, the love of Our Lord Jesus Christ!

Hell, purgatory, heaven: they all lie within the creature itself; in its more or less developed passions, the soul contains its hell, its purgatory, while in the virtues sanctified by the Beloved Master's Doctrine, it finds its heaven, its paradise, wherein its bliss resides.

And what other law will we seek, Christians in Christ, that better captures the divine mercy than that of the reincarnation of Spirits, which is a truth because it was confirmed by the Divine Master when He spoke to Nicodemus?

Is it not preferable, is it not more acceptable than that monstrous invention of hell and purgatory, in which only pain and eternal torment can exist for the sinful soul, for the delinquent Spirit?

Hell?

So then, would God, who condemns His creature to eternal suffering for a momentary fault, rank below you, who do not do that? Would His justice be lower than yours, which is carried out according to the degree of guilt, whereas His always punishes with eternal penalties?

No, that is not the truth!

There is no hell, no purgatory! There are no ordained places for the sacrifice of the Creator's children! Those places, I assure you, exist only in the human imagination, ready to attribute to the Deity the qualities of their own spirits.

Meanwhile, Roman Church representatives may tell me that my reasoning is false and baseless, for hell is not the Church's creation but a logical and undeniable deduction from what is found in the biblical texts.

But if logic were the prevailing factor in the minds of those who took upon themselves the duty to spread the light of Christianity across humanity, surely the Church's impetus would be different, and the fruits of proselytism in the name of Jesus, over these nineteen centuries, would be otherwise.

They may yet say: the notion of hell is found in biblical texts, which depict it through the fires of Gehenna and the outer darkness, where one hears the gnashing of teeth within that unending flame[25].

Yet we must be logical; we must, following Paul's counsel, move beyond the letter that kills and seek the spirit that gives life[26].

When Peter, head of His Church, asked Jesus how often he should forgive his brothers' failings and wondered if seven times would suffice, the Divine Master answered, as recounted by the evangelist Matthew[27] that he should not do so seven times, but seventy times seven.

And if that is so, how can we accept that Jesus, who counseled limitless forgiveness for sinners, could firmly declare to His disciples, in His divine conscience, the existence of hell, which is the negation of the Almighty's love and mercy?

Could a part exceed the whole, earthly love surpass heavenly love, or the creature's mercy be greater than that of its Creator?

This is the actual logic of the biblical texts; therefore, why not speak the truth?

Why argue systematically against one's own conscience? Is it not obvious to every mind capable of judging the Creator that the Divine Master was speaking in language suited to the people who heard Him?

Does it not stand to reason for those with true judgment of the Creator that the fire that never goes out is the fire of the Spirit's remorse, that the outer darkness is the darkness of the soul hardened in sin, and that Gehenna is none other than conscience itself, devouring the delinquent Spirit in its deepest and most profound decrees?

This is the truth, yet it does not suit that souls be persuaded of it, since it is necessary to terrify them in order to preserve the status quo of nineteen centuries, which benefits not the true church, but certain individual interests!

Studying and meditating on the Gospel to extract from it the essence of Our Lord Jesus Christ's doctrine in spirit and truth, teaching it, and above all living by it, are indeed difficult tasks; and so, across humankind, we either find simple and unlearned Spirits who obey the laws of the Gospel, not for their essence but out of the fear they instill, or, for the more advanced Spirits—those better prepared—there arises a need to create new religions, new philosophical systems that more satisfactorily respond to human reason.

Meanwhile, it is you, priests, who are the tenants of the vineyard!

---

[25] Matthew, Chapter III, verse 12. Matthew, Chapter VIII, verse 12. Matthew, Chapter XIII, verses 49 and 50. Luke, Chapter XIII, verse 28.
[26] 2 Corinthians, Chapter III, verse 6.
[27] Chapter XVIII, verses 21 and 22.

You are now, today, the Spirits of the great parable[28] of the Divine Master, having been entrusted with the highest ministry—representing our God, our Creator, on Earth!

The prophets came to speak to humanity through the inspiration of its noblest, and by condemning idolatry, opposing baser instincts, they sought to turn Earth into the true paradise of Adam's legends; you, the tenants, the orthodox, the Church's priests, put them to death! Then came yet more missionaries to awaken your conscience, but they, too, were stoned and derided, banished from the face of the Earth, until the Creator, by His infinite mercy, sent His own Son! However, fearing that He might assume that authority in His divine hands which had been given to you, you priests, the orthodox, the doctors of the law, just as you had done with the earlier Spirits, took Him to the Cross, to ignominy and scorn.

But the time draws near, and the Divine Lord needs to know the labor of the vineyard's tenants.

He must know its yield, and if neither the prophets nor His own Son persuaded the wicked workers to fulfill their duty, He will seize from them the vineyard He had entrusted to their care and give it to other workers more worthy and faithful.

Behold Spiritism, present all over the Earth, gaining ground bit by bit in the yard and in the sowing fields! There it is, the forerunner of the Spirit of Truth, contending for possession of consciences, bringing to souls an understanding of the Beloved Master's true doctrine, and showing humanity the meek, most beloved Lamb of the Almighty who, in His love, in His affection, in His divine mercy, measured out no limits to sacrifice to atone for our sins!

There is Spiritism, clergymen, openly telling you—setting aside the honorable exceptions I mentioned in another chapter—that you constantly distort your priestly duty, for you have been far more concerned with giving Caesar what belongs to Caesar than with giving God what belongs to God. By trying to serve two masters, without actually serving either, you mold the sacred texts to your convenience and personal needs!

And so, once again, you take up the stones for stoning the prophets; once more you take up the Cross for the crucifixion of Our Lord Jesus Christ; anew you present yourselves, after nineteen centuries, as whitened sepulchers[29], in the pompous display of your monuments and

---

[28] Matthew, Chapter XXI, verses 33 to 46. Mark, Chapter XII, verses 1 to 12. Luke, Chapter XX, verses 9 to 19.
[29] Matthew, Chapter XXIII, verses 27 and 28. Luke, Chapter XI, verse 44.

your priestly robes, not realizing that the Spirit of Truth searches your consciences and, discerning the impurity hidden within your souls—impurity that whitewash cannot conceal—prepares and hastens the moment when you will be removed from that vineyard that can no longer be yours, due to your indolence and your distortion of Christian truths fully grasped by the majority of Spirits.

After talking to His disciples in that parabolic language about the vineyard—which I, perhaps somewhat harshly, have applied to modern times—Jesus was approached by the Sadducees who, not believing in the resurrection, raised the question of whose wife, on the day of resurrection, would a woman be if she had married multiple times[30].

The Divine Master seized the occasion to once again affirm that what is born of the flesh is flesh and what is born of the Spirit is Spirit; He answered them that the children of this age marry men to women, but at the day of resurrection there would be neither men nor women, for in God's presence all would be Spirits, all would be brethren.

From this simple and concise reply of Jesus, we see clearly that gender is a mere incident of the flesh and that those Spirits who achieve true resurrection shall no longer concern themselves with such things, which die and vanish with their earthly lives.

Those who cannot comprehend any love other than that of the flesh do not understand Our Lord Jesus Christ; only those who seek in impure instincts the flower of that noble sentiment can ponder marriage beyond death and life—in short, those who allow carnal passions to rule.

But how shall one rise again, how not see eternal death, if we deny reincarnation?

Or better yet, how could the Spirit taste eternal death and yet rise again, as the Holy Scriptures so insist?

This question finds an easy answer when we consider resurrection, in the sense the Divine Master gave it, as the soul's simple passage from the dominion of the flesh to the dominion of the spirit—a transition that shall occur as many times as one fails to abide by one's Creator's laws.

However, those who manage to arise from the flesh imbued with the virtues taught by the Divine Master—those in whose souls the seeds gifted by the Creator have sprouted beneath the gentle breath of

---

Acts of the Apostles, Chapter XXIII, verse 3.
[30] Matthew, Chapter XXII, verses 23 to 30. Mark, Chapter XII, verses 18 to 25. Luke, Chapter XX, verses 27 to 36.

Our Lord Jesus Christ—shall not return to taste the laws of death, and, leaving behind the flesh and the instincts that belong to it, they might indeed encounter not seven wives but seventy times seven wives, regarding them only as loving Spirits, loving with the angels' love—fraternal Spirits in the fraternal bond of heaven, embodied in that sublime teaching found in that beautiful poem spoken by Our Lord Jesus Christ beside Jacob's well, as He spoke to the Samaritan woman[31].

As Sacred History recounts, after Solomon's reign, when the kingdom of Israel was established under its first ruler, Jeroboam, the tribes of Judah and Benjamin broke away from the other ten tribes by choosing Solomon's son, Rehoboam, as their legitimate leader.

Immediately, a fierce religious dispute erupted between the kingdom of Judah and the kingdom of Israel, which persisted until the time of Our Lord Jesus Christ's appearance on Earth.

By definitively separating from the tribes of Judah and Benjamin, Jeroboam abolished the worship of Jehovah and made new gods for the adoration of the people he ruled; the tribe of Judah, guided by Solomon's son, upheld the Mosaic laws for some period of time, naturally developing a stern contempt for its idolatrous brethren, as the biblical texts relate—indeed, they had no dealings with each other and would not even exchange greetings.

Each believed itself to possess the truth: the people of Israel built their temple for the revelations of their worship; the people of Judah, for their part, had their own site of veneration, and thus developed that state of religious dissension in which every mind was firmly intransigent—until the coming of Our Lord Jesus Christ, who, by asking the Samaritan woman for water, instructs her:

— Give me something to drink, said the Divine Master; and the woman, deeply astonished, asked how He, being a Jew, could request water from a Samaritan.

— If you knew who is asking you for a drink, you would ask Me instead, and I would give you living water.

— How, Lord? the woman asked. The well is deep and You have nothing with which to draw the water! Are You perhaps greater than our father Jacob who gave us this well, from which he himself, along with his family and his livestock, drank?

— Whoever drinks of this water will thirst again, answered the Divine Master, but whoever drinks of the water that I give shall never

---

[31] John, Chapter IV, verses 5 to 14.

thirst, and that water will become within him a fountain springing up to eternal life.

As we see, this scene with the Beloved Lamb was but a pretext to teach humanity about the principles of true brotherhood; it was nothing more than a pretext to declare to the peoples of that time, as well as to those of today, that there are no fixed places for God's worship—neither on the Samaritans' mountain nor in the temples of Jerusalem.

Jesus seized that moment to tell all humankind, behind the veil of literal words, that the true temple, the true church, is the human heart, and that the depths of the soul are the true tabernacle from which the creature draws the incense of prayer in the fragrance of the flower of noble sentiments, rising toward its Creator and Our Lord Jesus Christ, the guide, protector, and governor of this planet.

No, Jesus did not conceive—nor can we—that those rendering worship and homage to a Creator would hate their peers, their equals, over a simple difference of outward religious practices. He did not consider that one who sincerely believes in God but violates the edicts of true fellowship could, by mere religious formulas, anathematize and condemn their brothers, instead of seeking to win them through their virtues, their Gospel-based morality—in short, through all those qualities that bring a person respect, admiration, and the regard of their fellows.

Jesus, a Jew, asked water of the Samaritan woman; in other words, Jesus wholly disavowed the dissension that existed at that time between the two peoples; thus, logically, He cannot fail to disavow today the rifts between the existing churches, for one of two things must be true: either those churches do not shelter within them any faithful who, above all external forms of worship, hold fast to Our Lord Jesus Christ's holy doctrine; or they are devoid of the Gospel sentiment and therefore bound to disappear, making way for the true church of which the Divine Master spoke to the Samaritan woman when He said: The time is coming when the peoples will worship God neither in Jerusalem nor on the mountain, but will understand that God is spirit and must be worshiped in spirit.

God is spirit; God is intelligence; God is thought; God is the fluid that governs all the fluids filling Nature. Let us not make God incarnate, for we cannot imagine His bodily form.

God is spirit, and we, as Spirits, must strive to draw nearer to this great Creative Center, along the Milky Way shown to us by Jesus in His earthly sojourn, kindling within our souls the noble sentiments bestowed upon us, so that we may partake of that boundless bliss—that paradise we lost when we ate of the fruit of sin.

God is spirit, and let us not be deceived: outward worship is but a mask the Spirit devises to conceal the ugliness within its ego; it is the whitewash on the sepulcher that outwardly beautifies the person, leaving, inside, the decay and corruption that cannot escape the penetrating eye of Our Lord Jesus Christ, despite all the whitewash in the world.

When humanity truly grasps the Master's words—sweep and adorn your houses; when it understands that nothing is hidden from God and that, no matter the formulas we contrive, the spirit shall always be what it really is; when humanity learns that the only genuine and worthy worship we can offer the Creator is the worship of good sentiments, and that in the public square as in the intimacy of one's room, God's eyes are upon us, for He is everywhere—then, on that day, there will be neither temples of Jerusalem nor Samaritans' mountains, because man will be convinced that his body is the true church where his Spirit withdraws into contemplation of the infinite, ascending, through constant effort, to reclaim the pure essence of the joys once lost but which Jesus, good, meek, and loving, has again brought him in the holy promises of His love, so fully manifested in the pages of His Gospel.

When humanity has embraced all these truths, the wall of pride that even now separates Samaria's children from Israel's children will vanish forever, and then the true disciples of Our Lord Jesus Christ will sit by Jacob's well to offer, with no distinction of race or creed, the blossom of their affections to all their brothers before God and Jesus.

I am the resurrection and the life, said the Beloved Lamb in this poem of light and love. I am the resurrection and the life means: those who follow my holy doctrine, those who willingly drink the bitterness of my experience, those who comprehend the words of my Gospel, shall rise to eternal life, never again encountering the shadows of death, for I am the light, I am the truth, I am the life.

And assuredly, JESUS IS THE RESURRECTION, JESUS IS THE TRUTH, JESUS IS THE LIFE!

CHAPTER V

Jesus is the resurrection and the life. — Healing of the paralytic by the pool of Bethesda. — The Sabbath day, according to the Mosaic law. — The true fast. — Multiplication of the loaves and fishes.

"I am the resurrection and the life," said Our Lord Jesus Christ; the resurrection and the life, unfortunately still not understood by those who have embraced His holy doctrine.

Speaking to the Samaritan woman, the Most Loving Master was not referring to the resurrection of the flesh, as the Jews understood, but to the rising of the sinful soul, to the release of the erring Spirit from the chains of matter into true life—the life of the spirit.

That is the only understanding we can give to the lesson of the Divine Master, provided we seriously meditate on the words of the Gospel. To rise, to have life, to progress, ceaselessly seeking the object of all one's aspirations—such is the destiny of the creature, such the will of the Creator, such the desires of the Divine Master!

To rise again, never to taste death—that is, never again to return to the sepulcher of the flesh to atone for crimes and faults from past existences—this is the truth the Divine Lamb taught when He said: "I am the resurrection and the life; whoever believes in Me, whoever follows My doctrine, exemplifying it through the ceaseless practice of love for one's neighbor, shall never taste death."

And by believing in Jesus, understanding His doctrine, and finally embracing it, is man not truly freed from death, ascending once more to his lost paradise, where he must enjoy that holy and indefinite bliss which is the inheritance of the good?

Yes, certainly; but how will we obtain that blessing for which we dream during the hours of the Spirit's rest, forgetting the struggles of material life? How will we free ourselves from the chains of sin so as to achieve it?

Simply by having faith, having hope, and having will!

We are like paralytics by the Sheep Pool—Bethesda—into whose depths we long to descend for the healing of our afflictions[32]. We surely lack action and movement; but if hope exists within us, if we have will, if faith sustains us, we shall have at our side, as nineteen centuries ago, the Divine Lamb, who will, by giving us His hand as He did for the paralytic, say to us: "Rise and walk!"

Those who, at every moment, at every instant, know how to have faith and how to have will, are prepared to rise from inertia and have the movement of the spirit, for faith—that unconquerable force, that mighty lever which, in Our Lord Jesus Christ's words, can move mountains—restores man, elevating him to his God, his Creator and Father!

But, in raising the paralytic, did Jesus perform a miracle? Did He override the laws of nature?

And—free-thinkers will ask—then, to restore the health of the chronically ill, is a mere word enough?

And what would be easier, men of science: is it easier to form planets, with all the physical properties that you know and admire, or merely to act fluidically upon bodies that have grown cold and inert, giving them healing, which is movement and action?

If we consult Holy Scripture, we find Jesus performing healings through the action of the law of fluids, and never working miracles by overriding the laws established by the Creator; this is why we do not see Him restoring missing limbs to a body that had lost them.

What He did belonged to the realm of the law of fluids, which men, ignorant of it, considered supernatural; and it will remain so until the time comes for the mysteries to be revealed, mysteries that the limited scope of human intellect cannot yet grasp, but which they will eventually reach once they are freed from the leprosy of sin, through the constant practice of the Divine Model's teachings, and can receive the light that radiates from the pages of His Gospel!

Jesus gave sight to the blind whose iris was atrophied; He restored speech to the mute whose vocal cords were atrophied; in short, He healed the sick—though of curable conditions—simply by the imposition of fluids, which He knew as Governor of this planet and

---

[32] John, Chapter V, verses 1 to 16.

over which He had absolute authority throughout all Nature.

And these facts, attested by the Gospels, if ever challenged by scientists, will not be challenged in good faith, for no one is permitted to deny the laws of magnetism, which are now perfectly known; no one can reject the science of hypnotism, which has already found recognition from the learned of the Earth.

The fluid is the universal agent; and if, as is now proven and indisputable, man—who is but a sinner—can use it for the treatment of certain specific diseases, how can one in all sincerity deny the cures called miraculous, effected by Our Lord Jesus Christ, who, being not man and far less a sinner, performed them in His domain by employing, through the power of His will, the laws of charity and love, in order to demonstrate proofs of faith?

If the simple will of a wretched creature, riddled with imperfections, can—supported by ardent faith in the mercy of his Creator—summon fluids capable of bringing relief to the pains of a fellow man, what then could not be done by the mighty will of the pure and immaculate Son of Mary?

Yet the Jews deemed the Divine Master worthy of reproach for choosing the Sabbath day—consecrated to rest—to command the poor invalid to pick up his bed once He had healed him.

He, who had the power to raise the paralytic, just as He had the power, even while far from the official's son in Capernaum, to restore him to life at the mere decree of His sovereign will[33], was deemed, in the eyes of the Jews, to have no right to use the Sabbath day for acts of charity!

Feeble-minded spirits, without sufficient development to understand, in spirit, the provisions of Mosaic law went so far as to consider good deeds a crime!

Such were their purely worldly preoccupations; so focused were they on the constant pursuit of material interests that Moses deemed it necessary to decree at least one day on which, leaving aside material life and the concerns of base gain, they could devote a few moments to the worship of Jehovah; and, to lend the law greater force, he gave as its reason what is found in Genesis, namely that God rested on the seventh day of Creation.

Today, however, now that the light comes to illuminate our Spirit, today that truth is partly known to men, we can better understand than the Jews of old that, just as there are no specific days for worshiping

---

[33] John, Chapter IV, verses 46 to 54.

Jehovah, there are likewise no days forbidden for the practice of good.

At every moment, at every instant, in the toils of his earthly life, man must pray; for it is not the body but the Spirit that prays, and the Spirit, whatever posture the flesh may adopt, must ever be detached, seeking its Creator, seeking its Divine Master, to whom it owes the immense harvest from which it gathers the abundant fruits of love and faith, charity and peace.

Today we understand that every day, at every moment and every instant, we must do good by practicing charity toward our neighbor—the finest prayer we can offer before the Almighty—so that daily, at every moment and every instant, He may pour on us, as a consoling balm upon our sorrows, the blessings of His mercy and His infinite love!

But were the Jews sincere in the reproach they leveled against the Divine Master?

Were they truly scandalized by seeing Him, by doing good on the Sabbath, profane the laws of Moses?

No; they needed only a pretext to lead the most loving of Spirits to the ignominy of the cross.

From the laws of Moses, the scribes and Pharisees took hold of whatever was most severe and unyielding, applying it to mankind, and disregarded the dictates of love, charity, and fraternity, which for them lay lifeless in the law.

And that is why the Divine Master, accused by the Jews, replied, as recorded in John, Chapter V: "If you truly believed Moses, you would believe Me, because he wrote of Me;" meaning, "If you were sincere protectors of the doctrine of the great prophet, you would not seek a pretext in Caesar's coin nor in the Sabbath day to lead your Brother to the cross merely for doing good!"

Today, to be sure, no one is condemned for doing good on this or that day, yet there are still criticisms for anyone who, on certain days, fails to observe the laws of fasting.

But does that fast find any justification in the New Testament, in the Good News of Our Lord Jesus Christ?

If we study the Holy Scriptures, searching in Matthew, Chapter XVII, Mark, Chapter II, Luke, Chapter V[34], for a spiritual and truthful understanding of the teachings they contain, can we in any way agree with the practice established on that matter by the church of our day?

---

[34] Matthew, Chapter XVII, verses 14 to 21. Mark, Chapter II, verses 18 to 22. Luke, Chapter V, verses 33 to 39.

Certainly not.

Thus, when Jesus heard the reproach made by the Pharisees and scribes against His disciples for not observing this law, He replied that they did not need to fast at that time because they had the bridegroom with them. Then, so as still to teach beneath the veil of the letter a lesson against that practice—which no longer had any reason to be— He declared that no sensible and prudent man should put a patch of new cloth on an old garment, nor new wine in old wineskins, lest both be lost.

When Jesus said to His disciples and to the Pharisees that He had not come to destroy the law but only to fulfill it, He was referring to the law itself, to God's law received by Moses, which in all ages had to be fulfilled since its origin was superior and divine. But those laws which, though inspired in the Hebrew legislator, were adapted only to the times and customs of those peoples, these were assuredly meant, by the natural course of evolution, to be replaced once, with the coming of Jesus to Earth, they no longer had any reason to exist.

Thus, fasting, like circumcision and many other rites of that time, constituted—within the veiled thought of the Divine Model—the old cloth, the old wineskin that could not contain the spirit of reform carried by His Good News, because Spirits, obeying natural law, had progressed, and new horizons had opened to their understanding through the words of God's Messenger. It was therefore not possible for such laws—intended solely to address the needs of the people to whom they were given—to fit into His doctrine and His new teachings. And His disciples could not observe them without misrepresenting what the Divine Master intended, namely, to give new shape to beliefs and new foundation to faith, gathering humanity into a single center of light to guide it along the paths of progress and salvation.

That is why, under the veil of the letter, the Most Loving Lamb clearly teaches that the sensible and discerning person must not parade their religious convictions, testifying to their true belief through purely material practices which cannot benefit the spirit, for they belong to the realm of the flesh.

To the disciples who, in astonishment, drew near the Divine Master to ask why they had been unable to free a wretched brother who was possessed by a demon, the Divine Lamb said to them: "Because that kind of spirit is driven out only through much fasting and prayer!"

And we ask in turn: could enlightened reason in any way admit, could simple common sense conceive, that Our Lord Jesus Christ gave His disciples a teaching by which they should withhold material food necessary to the functioning of the body?

But then, would it suffice to mortify the body—that is, deprive it of what it intrinsically needs—so that the Spirit might ascend to that lofty realm of faith, which alone accomplishes the great works of charity?

Is it enough to afflict the body for the Spirit to gain that sense of love of neighbor which embodies the blessed prayers that rise up to the feet of the Lord as pleas of mercy for the unfortunate?

But if it is true that it is not what enters the mouth that makes a person unclean, but what comes out of the heart, why not understand, in spirit and truth, that the fast recommended by the Divine Master is wholly spiritual? Why not grasp that it consists solely in refraining from evil deeds, which lower the Spirit in the eyes of its Creator, so that, by repenting at every moment, one will not repeat errors and transgressions for which one repents?

And yet it is taught to Christendom that, to be right with God, one need only abstain from certain earthly foods! Moreover, by selecting which substances a person may consume, some are forbidden while others are permitted, in order to ease consciences that often wrestle in a cycle of imperfections and sins, as though these could be absolved by the deprivation or choice of food, when indeed the flesh avails nothing, and only beautiful sentiments and great virtues can make a true Christian love God above all things and love his neighbor as himself, revering the beacon of his hopes—the Blessed Son of Mary!

No, Christians; the fast Our Lord Jesus Christ has been asking of you for nineteen centuries is the abstention from your crimes, your daily sins; it is your true form of penitence, so that you may remain steadfast in your feelings once you have the fortune to open your hearts to receive, in the chalice of the bloom of your remorse, the dews of divine mercy!

This is the true fast, and blessed is he who understands it so and puts it into practice!

After giving this sublime teaching to His disciples and the people around Him, the Divine Master multiplied the loaves and fishes to satisfy the hunger of both body and spirit for a great multitude that sought Him, yearning for wonders and miracles to strengthen their belief and faith that He was indeed the awaited Messiah[35].

But—say the strong-minded—how could Jesus multiply the loaves

---

[35] Matthew, Chapter XIV, verses 14 to 21. Mark, Chapter VI, verses 34 to 44. Luke, Chapter IX, verses 12 to 17. John, Chapter VI, verses 1 to 15.

and fishes if fish, in their formation, follow preestablished laws of Nature? How absurd is the doctrine His believers and disciples would foist upon us?!

Indeed, the scholars, these extraordinary intellects of the century, know all of Nature!

And if they have not yet formed worlds, it is undoubtedly because they have not wished to do so; if they have not created the smallest insect, it is because they have not yet found time!

That is why, Christians in Christ, the Divine Master surrounded Himself with humble fishermen; that is why He chose, as continuators of His great and extraordinary work of regeneration, the humble and the small!

The doctors of the law in those times, just like the intellectuals of today, could not have comprehended Jesus, for they lacked that delicate instinct—the purity of soul revealed by one's gaze, a hallmark of the meekness of the just!

They lack the virtues of humility, which can restrain their prideful impulses! You, however, Christians in Christ, in your spiritual smallness, though clothed in the rags of your mental poverty, can understand—without being scholars—that everything in Nature is fluid, and that therefore the organization of bodies is effected by the combination of those very fluids. If those bodies, by the law of decomposition, eventually return to the great laboratory of Nature, then it is clear that Our Lord Jesus Christ, the Word of God, God's very Thought, who wields absolute power, held in His hands all the elements of their composition whenever He deemed it right to humble the arrogance and vanity of men.

Everything is fluid, I repeat; everything in Nature is magnetism. Should there be a single fact that disproves what I assert, in light of the biblical texts, it is merely your ignorance!

There was thus no miracle, if by miracle we mean, as the orthodox do, an overriding of natural laws.

Moreover, how can you claim these laws to have been overridden when you do not know them?

And how could you know them, if pride blinds your eyes?

Would you understand these truths? Come down from the heights of your learning to the humility of the fishers of souls; only thus will you succeed!

Study the new revelation, come forth to meet the Spirit of Truth, and by giving your mind repose, set your heart to work. Reflect on tomorrow, which may surprise you, for the Beloved Disciple said in his

Divine Epic: "The spirit is everything, and the flesh profits nothing." And you, who are Spirits and cannot do without the nourishment required by your spiritual nature, before you are caught unawares by a future you disregard, you must ever ask—today and always—for THE BREAD OF LIFE, WHICH IS THE IMMACULATE LAMB, OUR BLESSED MASTER!.

CHAPTER VI

The flesh and blood of Our Lord Jesus Christ. — Promises and offerings, according to the Church of Rome. — The parable of the barren fig tree. — The oath before the Gospel. — The Syllabus. — Idolatry. — The succession of St. Peter's chair. — The commerce of images. — To the dead befalls the burial of the dead. — The intolerance of the Roman Church.

I am the bread of life, and if you eat of it, you shall never be hungry; it is necessary that my flesh and my blood be your nourishment, for my flesh is truly food and my blood is truly drink.

In these words, under the veil of the letter, the Divine Master confirms the truth of what I said regarding His body in Chapter I of this humble work.

— My body is truly food, my blood is truly drink; if you do not eat of my body and if you do not drink of my blood, you shall not be saved.

Hearing these truths, many of those who surrounded the Divine Lamb grumbled: This speech is hard, and we cannot understand it[36]!

And why could they not understand it?

Because they sought in these words the letter and only the letter, when they should have sought to interpret them in spirit and truth, disregarding the material objective that they absolutely did not contain.

The flesh of Jesus, the blood of Jesus, was His doctrine; and man, famished for love and thirsty for faith, was to eat of this flesh and drink of this blood!

And that apparent human body had to be delivered to the fury of the scribes so that, from His pains, from His martyrdom, those great

---

[36] John, Chapter VI, verses 47 to 61.

sowings would burst forth on the surface of the Earth, from which His brothers would reap the sweet fruits of love, faith, and charity.

His speech was indeed harsh; and, because many who heard it did not comprehend it, they withdrew from the Divine Master, leaving Him with His twelve apostles, His sincere friends, those on whom He could rely for the grand work of human regeneration, spreading everywhere the lights of His Good News, which one day would be translated into the sublime apotheosis of His glory, through the concretion of sentiments refined in the crucible of His divine doctrine—a doctrine which, in times to come, will constitute the greatest proof, the greatest testimony, of the truth He taught, namely that everything on Earth would pass away, except His words!

Human brotherhood—this is the ultimate aim of the doctrine of Our Lord Jesus Christ! But to achieve this result, it is necessary for the true Christian to know and practice the teachings of the Beloved Master, and, to that end, it is incumbent on me to seek in the resplendent pages of the Gospel that glorious spirit concentrated therein, so that I may present it to Christendom as a sure guide for its destiny.

And even if some suspect that this humble book's sole purpose is to combat Catholicism, I shall persist to the end, even hurting consciences, because I observe in my brothers—on whose shoulders weighs the arduous task of guiding peoples along the paths of the religion of Our Lord Jesus Christ—certain distortions of the sound principles of evangelical morality; I note that day by day they are losing that precious ground their forefathers managed to conquer in man's conscience. And, amid the frenzy and delirium of a spirit that cannot conform to ritualistic formulas, I observe a powerful surge in thought, giving rise to philosophical schools of inconceivable extravagance, which are accepted by that eager Spirit seeking in them something to satisfy its reason and intelligence.

I do not have the firm intention, let me say, of attacking Catholicism itself, nor the Roman practices; but only, by opening before Christendom the Gospel of Our Lord Jesus Christ, to show it what is error, what is truth, where to find the light radiating from the true teachings of the Divine Master, and how to avoid the darkness cast upon them by the grafts men have made.

I have fought against fasting; I have criticized baptism which, by the manner in which it is celebrated, cannot signify acceptance of the doctrine of Our Lord Jesus Christ by the one who receives it. I have fought against the marketplace of the sacraments, just as I shall fight against promises, because all these things are pure and simply the distortion of the Beloved Master's doctrine.

And if these external forms, these practices of the Roman Apostolic Catholic Religion, satisfy less discerning souls, nevertheless, in the mind of the thinking individual, they carve a profound chasm, with the result that philosophical schools arise to combat what we hold most sacred, striking at what is most precious and holy to our spirit—the Gospel of Our Lord Jesus Christ, to whom we owe our salvation.

When He said to His disciples—I am the bread of life—and offered His body and His blood for the salvation of creatures, the Divine Master exhorted them not to offend their neighbor, not even by the slightest word. He insisted on this, saying further: Make peace with your adversary while you are on the road with him in the world, lest it happen that, once departed, he should denounce you to the judge, thus having you suffer the immediate condemnation of your instincts of hatred and rancor! And when you go to make your offering, before laying it on the altar, consult your conscience, and if it tells you that one of your brothers has reason to complain against you, seek him out, reconcile yourself with him, so that then you may fulfill your duty[37].

From this sublime and divine counsel of Jesus, we see that the creature cannot bring to its Creator a greater offering than the love it dedicates to its neighbor; that fraternity is the greatest testimony man can offer God of the belief and faith awakened in his sinful soul by the sweet and merciful word of the pure and immaculate Son of Mary.

Nevertheless, offerings are still brought before the altars; even today, the Church minister allows the flock to enter the fold without heeding the voice of their own conscience, simply because they bring something material to offer to God!

And thus, the Church's ministers, the representatives of Jesus on Earth—may they forgive me the expression—allow the bribery of the Divinity to obtain miracles that only true faith can produce!

And if faith is a dead letter, it suffices to enter into an agreement with the good Spirits so that we may exchange services with them; comforted in our conscience, we obtain from the Creator what we desire!

But how absurd all this is!

And is it not our duty, as Spiritists, to censure this, in the name of truly evangelical principles?

Yes, certainly!

---

[37] Matthew, Chapter V, verses 22 to 26.

Let us unite in a single thought, and by forming a truly Christian legion, let us strike hard and deeply at those abuses that distort the Beloved Master's doctrine; and in so doing, in the name of Our Lord Jesus Christ, we shall once more be, within the temples of Jerusalem, the voice protesting—invoking the Holy Gospels—against this marketplace that translates the corruption of the sound principles of Christian morality!

Those who think to obtain the so-called miracles by means of offerings deceive themselves!

They deceive themselves, indeed, because if God's mercy does not delay in coming to those who resort to it by taking shelter under the Divine Mantle of His blessed Son, it is certainly not for the value of the offering they bear to the altar but solely for the purity of intent of the sinful soul that, on the wings of fervent prayer, rises to the feet of the Creator, begging for balm for its pains and comfort for its sorrows!

It is faith and faith alone which, even if veiled by these material falsehoods, ascends to the spheres of light, obtaining the grace and mercies that God knows how to distribute to all His children, even the most sinful. Only in this way, by the purity of the soul's sentiments, is the pure, holy, and divine Spirit of God moved!

Seek, Christians, at all costs to develop within your souls that flower of pure sentiments that will inspire you toward true life, toward the happiness your Spirits yearn for. Cast aside these material formulas that have no place in the divine Code—the Beloved Master's Good News.

And if until now you have been the barren fig tree of the Gospel, take advantage—there is still time—of this new year the Lord grants you, drawing into the roots of your soul the sap of the teachings that Spiritism now brings you, so that you may secure your salvation.

Read the Gospel of Luke, Chapter XIII, and apply the parable of the fig tree to your own individuality[38].

The vineyard is the pitiable Earth on which you struggle, repairing the faults and sins of your past existences; you are the fig tree that must bear fruit—the fruits of love, faith, and charity. And if the planet, obeying the laws of progress, must take on new forms compatible with its conditions, then you, should you fail to produce the fruits the Lord demands of your Spirit, will be transplanted to inferior worlds, true hells, a true gehenna, from which you shall lament the paradise that you have relatively lost!

Jesus permits the Spirit of Truth to illuminate your souls, shaking

---

[38] Luke, Chapter XIII, verses 6 to 9.

your consciences; and, through His holy messengers, He calls you to the practice of Christian love.

Listen to Him; He is the bread of life—nourish yourselves with Him; He is the fountain that flows from eternity—drink, quench your thirst, concentrating within your souls that immeasurable treasure that, by the Father's grace, Jesus dictated to men!

I feel how painful is the duty that weighs upon my shoulders. I grasp the profound shock that these truths shall produce in consciences, truths that I am obliged to deliver to Christendom in my fervent effort to call it to serious meditation on the teachings of Our Lord Jesus Christ—teachings that may have been, who knows, intentionally hidden until now by those whose duty it was—even more than mine—to unfold, in all its light, the pages of that sacred book we call the Good News, and which was brought to Earth by the most loving of Spirits, for the love of men.

But if the times have come; if it is certain that the fig tree must necessarily produce the fruits that justify its permanence in the vineyard; and if every Christian in Christ has the duty to share with his brothers whatever light he may have received, so as to enlighten them on the path of their salvation, I feel perfectly justified, in my conscience, for touching, even if lightly, upon these points, thereby striking and unsettling those spirits not yet awakened to the truth.

Religious practices that lack sanction in the Gospel do not belong to the doctrine of Our Lord Jesus Christ.

Thus, those who call themselves His representatives on Earth either consider themselves superior to the Divine Model—enabling them to alter His teachings in letter and spirit, which is unacceptable—or they systematically graft onto the holy doctrine precepts that pervert its essence, committing a crime, for surely the Creator and Father did not grant them the sacred ministry for that reason, but rather so they might guide, in this world, the errant Spirits seeking their salvation.

By modifying the Mosaic laws, adapting God's true law to the society of His time, Jesus, among other teachings and precepts, counseled His disciples—indeed, all humanity—to swear not at all, neither by Heaven, nor by Earth, nor by the Temple of Jerusalem, nor by their own heads. Let your speech, He said, be yes, yes—no, no, for anything beyond this comes from evil.

That is found in Matthew, Chapter V of his Gospel, verses 33 and following[39].

---

[39] Matthew, Chapter V, verses 33 to 37.

The Gospel, wherein that great teaching is established, that very Gospel, serves as the basis for believers' oaths!

And so men swear upon the holy book, though that same book commands the Christian not to swear, but always to speak the truth in the light of his own conscience, before God and before men!

But we ask: can the true Christian, the one who regards the Gospel as the divine Code it is, take such an oath?

Certainly not. And why has the Church not protested, nor does it protest, against this abuse manifest in the Beloved Master's teachings?

Other concerns, which for her have greater value, occupy her time, rather than disseminating the truth contained in the Gospel of Our Lord Jesus Christ!

The thirst for domination, the manifest intolerance that on its own contradicts what the Divine Lamb taught, the Church's preoccupation with material things while neglecting those that concern the happiness of the Spirit—this is the real reason for the distortion of what is enshrined in the luminous pages of the book of our salvation!

Jesus was boundless love; Jesus was charity; Jesus was tolerance! He always strove to persuade His earthly brethren, never to vanquish them by force of His power, which, in fact, He possessed in superabundance!

Whether feasting at Simon the publican's table, or begging water from the Samaritan woman rejected by the Jews, He revealed Himself as a Spirit who loved conciliation, a soul open to true brotherhood, drawing no distinction between heretics or gentiles!

Yet, what do those who proclaim themselves His ministers on Earth practice?

They create the Syllabus—a law of iron that intends to constrain human thought, suppressing all those aspirations of the Spirit, no matter how noble! This code, which declares the Roman Apostolic Catholic Religion the only one for all states, to the exclusion of every other religion, treats the foreigner as a veritable slave who must not be allowed to practice the worship he professes!

The Syllabus which, among other outrages to the doctrine of Our Lord Jesus Christ, decrees that His vicar on Earth cannot be reconciled with, nor concede to, the spirit of liberalism or civilization!

But where does the Gospel of the Beloved Master sanction all these absurdities? On which page of the Divine Code will you find a single word authorizing these laws of intolerance that wholly deny the love of God and the teachings of Our Lord Jesus Christ?

And could they be, perhaps, instituted by a successor of Peter the fisherman, the apostle?

And would Peter—who drank in at the Beloved Master's side those great teachings of love and brotherhood—allow his successors to maintain doctrines that corrupt the Gospel?

Certainly not; it was not the successor of Peter who sanctioned these laws, just as it was not the successor of Peter who, despite the protests of true Christians, restored the worship of idols—which is nothing other than what is practiced in the Church today!

Oh! the truth must be spoken! Let Christendom and free-thinkers know that for six centuries the doctrine of Our Lord Jesus Christ prevailed on Earth, in a form wholly different from what is seen now!

The Church of Jerusalem, attended by Peter, was the model for all others; there, the Old and New Testaments were studied and pondered, preparing souls in that crucible of love so they might rise up to the sacred feet of their Creator and Father, by practicing the sublime teachings of the Beloved Master!

In the seventh century, the innovations emerged, perhaps when—worn out by serious meditations on the sacred writings—men deemed it necessary to return to the times before Our Lord Jesus Christ, restoring idolatry!

And it is indeed so true that Pope Gregory the Great[40], noticing such transgression, ordered all idols removed from the churches, rebuking the ministers who had allowed such a thing. Later, however, his successors Boniface III and IV not only reinstated the worship of idols but also deemed it a dogma of faith!

But Christians, if the Gospel teaches us that God is Spirit and that only in Spirit shall He be adored by those who truly worship Him[41]; if Peter received the mandate as head of the Church, and if for centuries those absurd practices remained unknown, how can we claim that the present-day Church is Peter's Church and represents the teachings of Our Lord Jesus Christ?

It is painful, truly painful, but it must be said: the present-day Church is the greatest affront to the Gospel and to the truth!

And though it may appeal to its right of succession to Peter's chair, I will ask the Church: To whom do you grant that succession?

To John XXIII[42] or to Benedict XIII, both deposed by the Council

---

[40] Born in Rome in 540 and died in 604; elected pope in 590. He reformed the liturgy; he is accused of having destroyed a great number of ancient manuscripts and monuments of pagan art.
[41] John, Chapter IV, verses 20 to 24.
[42] Baldassare Cossa, a native of Naples; elected pope in 1410 in Bologna, upon the death of Alexander V, by the vote of 16 cardinals, while others

of Constance[43], which ordered John Huss[44] to be burned alive? To Honorius I[45], anathematized by his successors?

To Gregory the Great, who condemned idol worship, or to Boniface III and IV, who restored said worship?

Peter was humble; Peter was love; Peter was faith; and for that reason, the Divine Master charged him with the great mission of founding His Church on Earth. He was the pilgrim who, from city to city, tribe to tribe, with his staff in hand and empty bag, carried his beloved Master's word, teaching souls the path to Heaven! Peter never possessed gilded palaces nor amassed millions while the poor were affronted; he never sold indulgences or relics of any kind for profit! And always keeping before his eyes the image of his dear Master expelling the merchants from the temple, he himself could never have been a merchant!

To his successors—that is, his disciples—he never passed down these formulas that distort, corrupt, and block the true path that Christendom must tread!

Had those who proposed to be his followers imitated his examples, which reflect the doctrine of Our Lord Jesus Christ, the Church would not be divided; all would partake at the same table, for truth is one and unique.

Had his pseudo-followers endeavored to mimic him, we Spiritists would not have to witness Christians adoring idols—though they should know that Christ condemned idolatry. We would not have to

---

recognized Peter de Luna as pope, under the name of Benedict XIII. He convened the Council of Constance, which deposed him in 1415; he was then imprisoned for three years. He died in Florence in 1419.

[43] Convened by an edict of Emperor Sigismund in 1413; it assembled in 1414 under the presidency of Pope John XXIII.

[44] Born in Bohemia in 1373; rector of the University of Prague in 1409. For his writings denying papal authority, censuring the clergy's vices, excommunications, indulgences, etc., he was excommunicated by Pope Alexander V. Appealing to the Council of Constance, he was declared a heretic there and, by order of that very council, was burned alive in 1415, in Constance.

[45] Pope from 626 to 628. Born in Capua, son of Consul Petronius. He was anathematized many years after his death at the Council of Constantinople; for centuries, popes could not ascend the throne without pronouncing an anathema in which they uttered the name of Honorius. The condemnation of a pope as a heretic is the best argument against infallibility. Father Gratry says: "The condemnation of Honorius is, and shall be, the eternal obstacle to the doctrine of infallibility."

behold the spectacle—before God and before human art—of commerce, a marketplace of figures or images which, in the words of the very priests, are mere dolls until sprinkled with holy water, itself but a simple imitation of the pagan lustral waters; nor would we see these processions in the public square that scandalously feature what they call the image of Our Lord Jesus Christ!

And how could it be otherwise, if the Church is divided and those cultivated Spirits cannot conform to such ridiculous practices that are imposed upon them by those who can represent anything on Earth except the doctrine of the Beloved Master?

If popes imitated Peter, if they were other such pilgrims with staff in hand and empty bags, we would certainly never see God's minister on Earth praying at the edge of a tomb where matter is corroding! And praying to whom? The flesh, to putrefaction?

Or does the priest ignore that at the moment of that phenomenon which men call death, the Spirit departs, and only by Spirit can we seek it with fervent prayer in the infinite realms?

And does the priest not know the Gospel teaches that to the dead befalls the burial of the dead[46]?

How, then, for the sake of vile coins, does the minister of Jesus pay homage to the flesh that corrupts?

If Peter's successors drank in at his side the Beloved Master's true teachings, in the so-called holy ground they would make no distinction. Rather, there they would level tombs, representing, before God, the equality of dust! Yet they do, caring about the little plot of land where the inert flesh that once clothed the Spirit is to lie; and again twisting the teachings of the Divine Model, they do not allow followers of a religion likewise akin to their own in its foundations, differing only in form, to rest there.

And, so zealous of matter, even in putrefaction, they fight against the secularization of cemeteries as though that were a great outrage in God's sight and before the Gospel!

And full of intolerance, they fail to mind the deep rift they create between the Church and those who think the free-thinkers, whose ideas they should not spurn, for it is not proper to rule over ignorance, to hold sway only over those who do not ponder, nor think, nor solve anything! And by so doing, instead of producing believers, they produce fanatics who, not grasping the absurdities of these rules and rites, submit to them blindly, without awareness of what they practice!

---

[46] Matthew, Chapter VIII, verses 21 and 22.

Thus, entering the necropolises, they admire the great mausoleums and, absorbed in contemplation, murmur their prayers, returning content to their hearths. The cultivated Spirits, however, the freethinkers, upon entering and not finding the tombs leveled, upon seeing the priest standing before a grand monument, praying in secrecy to a tomb that holds only corruption, venture yet farther, seeking the mass grave, where the killers' bodies lie pressed against the maidens' bodies. Then, raising their thoughts to Heaven, they exclaim: Lord of the unknown, am I wrong in not following the religion of Your Beloved Son, or is there some other religion overruling the true one that was lost in the silence of time?

And they return home, not with the fanatic's tranquility, but with souls locked in a titanic inner struggle between reason and sentiment, weighed down by a world of shadows and light, doubt and uncertainty, the immensity of it grieving their guides, whose mission is to accompany them through life's pilgrimage!

Christians in Christ, meditate upon the words of the Gospel, raise yourselves up, lifting your Spirits out of the mire of Earth: open your hearts to the divine light, summon from the depths of your souls the Spirit of Truth, and strive with all your might to ascend to the heights of light, so that you may comprehend the sublime teachings of the Divine Lamb, the only ones that can bestow upon you the happiness you so ardently desire, atoning for your sins.

There you have Spiritism; study it in the light of the Gospel, and in it you shall find the fountain that quenches your thirst, the bread from Heaven—Our Lord Jesus Christ!

But if you truly wish to taste that lifegiving water that soothes the believer's soul, if you hope to savor that bread from Heaven, symbolized by the doctrine of the Beloved Master, you cannot forego meditation on the Gospel; you cannot substitute for the essence of its divine teachings these formulas and conventions that the Spirit cannot accept without betraying the true principles of faith.

Seeking the water that quenches the thirsty soul of love and faith, seeking that bread from Heaven that nourishes the believer's Spirit so that he shall never again hunger for knowledge, is to look for Jesus in the silence of thought, away from the clamor of passions; it is to cast aside the material symbols said to personify Him, elevating the eyes of the soul to the infinite expanse, returning on the white wings of prayer to the ethereal mansions of the just, where dwells the most just of Spirits—the Savior of the world.

It is certainly not amid the dazzling splendor of great cathedrals, whose altars are ornamented with gold, silver, and precious stones so that sacrifices may be performed on them—sacrifices that differ only in form from those once celebrated in the temples of Jerusalem—nor in the silence of the confessional that we shall find the Most Loving Master, the Immaculate Lamb who condemned no one, not even the adulterous woman[47].

No; only in the Gospel—the holy ark of our salvation, that grand book which to this day has been kept out of Christendom's reach—shall we discover the Divine Master, for there alone His entire soul shines forth, drawing us to His most sacred bosom!

And let me say this, Christians in Christ: by an aberration of spirit, by man's wickedness, what you know the least about religion is precisely the Divine Code itself, the bedrock on which the entire edifice of the true Christian Church rests.

The books they fabricated, the ecclesiastical regulations, the dogmas, the pastoral letters—in short, that whole array of worldly things—none of this expresses, nor speaks to you of, the Good News, whose study and sincere meditation would enable you to find the true path, in the search for truth and in the just yearning for atonement for your sins!

And they have materialized everything, though matter was condemned by the Divine Master!

And for nineteen centuries the Spirit of Truth has descended into the heart of Christendom, finding there no love!

And for nineteen centuries the Spirit of Truth has sounded the hearts of those who call themselves believers, finding there no faith!

And the Christian family is divided by the prejudice of schisms, and the ministers of the Church focus on the transitory matters of the material world; leading conquering armies, they dig deep furrows of strife and discord in the heart of humanity. Pretending to serve religion in some capacity, they turn the sacred pulpit into a pillory from which they hurl to the crowd notions that run counter to the true doctrine, provoking the scandal foretold by the Most Loving Lamb and stirring in cultivated Spirits—if not hatred—at least indifference toward all that pertains to religion.

And how can one expect to find Jesus, the messenger of peace and love, when souls are drowning in this immense ocean of worldly passions?

How can one obtain God's mercy—who renders unto each

---

[47] John, Chapter VIII, verses 1 to 11.

according to his deeds—when the spirit is brimming with hatred for its neighbor?

Is it possible to find Jesus in a church that still teaches the doctrine of old—an eye for an eye, a tooth for a tooth—where one is counseled to love those who share our ideas and to hate those who reject them?

Would the Divine Nazarene be in a church that forbids prayer for the unfortunate soul who lacked the fortitude to endure the torments of this life?

Would He be in a church where intolerance reigns, where love and compassion are a dead letter, and which systematically persecutes a humanitarian society, whose members, for the most part, have raised cathedrals, enriching temples in the name of so-called religious orders?

Certainly not.

Jesus is everywhere two or three are gathered in His most holy name—the Gospel tells us[48]—but for you to be gathered in the name of Jesus, Christians in Christ, you must hold feelings akin, though not necessarily equal to those of the Divine Master. And it is surely not in the churches of this or that religion that you shall find the Divine Model, but rather in the tranquility of your own conscience, in the serenity of your Spirit, making of your believing soul a tabernacle from which you may behold the image of the Divine Nazarene reflecting upon you all the sweetness of His limitless love.

By the most sacred incense of your virtues, with the tears of your repentance—washing away your sins day by day, moment by moment,—only then shall you have close to you the One to whom you owe the fruitful harvest and to whom, one day, you must present the results of your love and gratitude.

There you have Spiritism, whose study and contemplation I once again invite you to undertake; but study it in the light of the Gospel, without concerning yourselves with the spectacular or with the satisfaction of material interests you may wish to obtain from it. Strive to understand it in spirit and truth, and therein you shall find the teachings of the promised Comforter, which embody the entire doctrine of the Beloved Master.

The times draw near; the hour of harvest is coming, and before the night of the tomb descends upon you with those surprises that bring despair to the soul, you must make use of the hours of daylight. Use them to cultivate the hard earth of your errors and imperfections, preparing yourselves so that you may rise again in the sweet and loving

---

[48] Matthew, Chapter XVIII, verses 19 and 20.

embrace of the Redeemer of the world!

Study the Gospel in the light of Spiritism, raising the edifice of your belief upon rock rather than shifting sands, for in this lies the foundation of your faith, the basis of your salvation; thus you will have attained Jacob's ladder for your ascent to the realms of light and truth.

Build the edifice of your belief upon rock—that is, understand and practice the Doctrine of Jesus, opening your soul to those pure sentiments that sanctify the angels.

If, however, you limit yourselves to reading the Gospel, to comprehending it without practicing it; if you remain steadfast and consistent with the laws of old, loving your friends and hating your enemies, you will have built on shifting sand, fulfilling your soul's needs with these precepts, these formulas of no value—treasures consumed by moths—possessions that decay, leaving your Spirits stripped of the true riches—the riches of Heaven!

CHAPTER VII

Spiritism in the light of the Gospels. — The law of reincarnation. — The eternity of punishment according to the Church of Rome. — The Great King's banquet. — Anathemas of the Catholic Church. — Parables of the adulterous woman and the prodigal son. — The Lord's Prayer. — Marriage and celibacy.

Inviting Christendom to the meditative study of Spiritism, in the light of the Gospel, I have chiefly in view diverting my brothers on Earth from the desire for marvels, which generally is what most concerns those who begin their study of the New Revelation.

Spiritism does not consist in this continual exchange of ideas with those who have departed from the transient life of matter, merely bringing man the intoxication of wonders that astonish the spirit, thirsty for the secrets of life beyond the grave.

No, absolutely not; it is a gift from Our Lord Jesus Christ and, as such, constitutes a holy and pure doctrine, whose practice fulfills a principle of usefulness for the peoples to whom the promise of the coming of the Comforter was made.

And just as, upon entering the Catholic temples, we investigate whether what goes on within them is in perfect accord with the Divine Code, the Gospel of our Redeemer, so too, in the workshops of spiritual work, let us inquire whether those who study Spiritism — the New Revelation — surely guide their actions by the precepts contained in the Good News.

And that is why we ask those who do not know it to try to learn about it through the Gospel.

If those who call themselves spiritists, if the inspired ones, do not practice the teachings that were given to them by the Redeemer as means of salvation; if — which would be monstrous — within the very workshops of spiritist labor a man can find, just as in the Catholic temples, Jerusalem's marketplace; if, through an obstinacy against true religious and Christian sentiment, spiritists have forgotten what is contained in the Gospel of Matthew, Chapter X, verse 8, then we can assert that in those centers there is not the light that Christendom needs in order to find once more the path from which it was diverted by ambition, by pride, by the tumult of passions that invaded the depths of the souls of those to whom was given the grand mission of spreading over the Earth the doctrine of Our Lord Jesus Christ.

We are not moved by the intention of attacking religions; we fight against the Catholic temple, just as we do the Protestant church, the Jewish synagogue, or the Mohammedan mosque, whenever we do not find in them, as the fundamental basis of all religious teaching, the love of God above all things and of one's neighbor as oneself.

Studying Spiritism, understanding it in spirit and in truth, is to search for the key to all the mystery of creation.

Studying this doctrine, understanding it, is to obtain the solution to those great problems of life that preoccupy every creature from the cradle to the grave.

And by studying and understanding it, in the blessed light of the Holy Gospels, Spiritism becomes enabled to free itself, on certain flights of the soul, from the swamps of earth into supreme happiness!

Through meditation upon it, man comes to know that, coming from a series of existences, he is the unclean larva passing through his crimes and errors until he finds in the Gospel the cocoon in which he must transform himself into a chrysalis for the garden of heaven!

And thus he gains an explanation for a number of facts that up until then seemed anomalous and absurd, finding support for his faith, shelter for his sorrows, a balm for his pains.

And the poor bless their poverty, and the humble laborer kisses the calluses that on his heavy hands appear to him as so many other focal points of the blessed light that must guide him on the journey to the unknown.

And the rich realize that everything a man possesses, except for wickedness, comes from God, and that therefore he must at least take from his surplus those things that will alleviate his brothers' sufferings, those Lazarus figures who, perhaps one day, will reach out their hands to show him Jesus.

And man begins to understand the Creator who, in the sacred pages of His Beloved Son's book, is revealed to him in all His splendor as the

God of love and mercy, as the Father who does not want the sinner's death but rather his salvation[49]. And so hell, that absurd creation of the Church, crumbles; in the believer's soul dawns the light of faith and hope in divine mercy, which assures him that not all is lost, however grave the sins committed; and, animated by these pure sentiments, the creature day by day, moment by moment, endeavors to free itself from the leprosy of sin, eyes fixed on the most holy image of the Divine Nazarene, beneath whose cloak of love it takes refuge, in search of the light that must illuminate the thorny road of its regeneration.

And man understands the law of reincarnation, the law of mercies, this sublime law by virtue of which the Spirit can rehabilitate itself indefinitely, understanding the great love of God for His creatures — love which, in turn, he must also distribute among his fellows through the boundless forgiveness of insults, slander, and wickedness, in short, that he has perhaps received from them.

But the Church's ministers will say that this doctrine of reincarnation is an absurdity; that such a law does not exist, and that in reality there are only hell, heaven, and purgatory; that the not-yet-purified souls prepare themselves, wherever it may be, for their ascent to heaven by the grace of the Lord, whereas the condemned descend to the depths of hell where the fires that never die out inflict on them suffering commensurate with their misdeeds!

The law of reincarnation does not exist! They would prefer it not to exist, that is what they should say, for there are many material interests harmed by the affirmation of this law and, therefore, it is indeed necessary to fight it, denouncing its proclaimers as mad or visionary.

To sincere Catholics, however, to men of good faith, I would offer an invitation to examine the biblical texts and then we shall see what sophistic approach must be adopted to distort the clear and positive message of Our Lord Jesus Christ concerning John the Baptist as the person of Elijah.

Was Elijah actually taken up bodily and spiritually to the regions of infinity, returning to Earth even if under another name, as the Church would have it?

And can we, perhaps, accept that statement as truth before the Gospel that reveals to us the mystery of the birth of John the Baptist through the sublime words with which the inspired Luke recounts how

---

[49] Ezekiel, Chapter XXXIII, verse 11. 2nd Epistle of Peter, Chapter III, verse 9.

the precursor quivered in Elisabeth's womb when the Immaculate Virgin Mother approached her[50]?

Let us open the Gospel of Matthew, Chapter XI, verses 13 to 15, and Chapter XVII, verses 10 to 13, and see that there is no need to invert the meaning of Jesus, which He expressed when His disciples asked Him about the coming of Elijah. He told them that Elijah had already come and that John the Baptist, if they chose to understand it rightly, was the same Elijah; and whoever had ears to hear should hear!

Here, then, is the doctrine supported by doctrine; the law grounded in the Gospel, according to an affirmation of the Divine Master, which constitutes a truth that no one is entitled to doubt!

And was this event, by chance, an exception?

Surely not, for an exception belongs to man, to humanity, and not to God.

The law is one and the same; what happened with Elijah has taken place since the dawn of humanity, for the Spirit experiences death many times, doing so because its errors drive it back into the prison of matter, where it must regenerate itself.

And now, men of good faith, sincere Catholics, tell me: where is there more of God, more mercy, more justice, and more love — in this doctrine forged by men, according to which the creature is condemned to an eternity of suffering for its momentary wanderings, closing its heart to the consoling hope of one day receiving, as a lenitive for its pain, the sweet and merciful light that radiates over all who suffer from the sacred bosom of Our Lord Jesus Christ; or in that other doctrine, which consoles and comforts us with the certainty that one day, redeemed by our own efforts, we shall have another, better life, the true life, in which we shall enjoy the supreme happiness?

Where is God more present: in the Gospel we study as madmen and visionaries, yet seeking to know the truth and nothing but the truth, or in that mound of books, of papal bulls, and of autos of the Holy Office that offers man, when he most needs relief from the thirst that consumes him, when he most requires compassion from his peers, when that hope should truly blossom in his soul, only the eternal flames of hell and the eternity of punishment for the sins of a moment?!

Study, Christians, the Gospel; prepare your spirit so that you may follow me to Calvary, where we can find the true Jesus!

In inviting sincere Catholics, men of good faith, to seek out the true Jesus, the blessed shepherd of souls — concealed from Christendom

---

[50] Luke, Chapter I, verses 39 to 45.

by the malice of men — it is timely to recall the divine parable found in Luke, Chapter XIV, verses 16 to 24, in which, beneath the veil of the letter, the Divine Master invites the poor and crippled to human fellowship, to the divine banquet that shall one day be presided over by the Most Loving Lamb — He who was predestined to suffer in His divine Spirit all the sorrows and misfortunes of wretched humanity[51].

The times draw near; to men who have been granted an existence on Earth, certainly not for the pleasures of the flesh but for the preparation of their Spirit and the purification of their soul, with a view to attaining supreme happiness, the magnificent invitation to the Great King's feast is extended once again; and woe to them if, perchance, citing material interests, they fail to show up!

Jesus founded His church, making the great Apostle Peter its spiritual head; thus, from that time onward, the rich board of divine communion was prepared, at which those who, being the first to request it, had obtained the alms that divine mercy denies to no one, were to take their seats. But individual interests provided excuses that led them to abandon the seat that awaited them at the feast, and, worse still, they harmed it with the clamor of their passions and with their greedy cries, deafening those who, having understood well the invitation being offered, might have come together to gladly receive the bread of life — the only nourishment distributed at this all-spiritual banquet!

But as time goes by, everything passes, everything vanishes; the word of Jesus, though at times distorted, prevails eternally, for it represents the truth, and truth is eternal!

The time of reparation has come; we must speak openly to Christendom, reviving in man's memory that splendid parable that has, since the earliest days, conveyed the most sublime affirmation of God's mercy for His creatures.

And you, Christians, do not deceive yourselves by trying to cast a veil over your reason, for belief, a faith that does not stand on that great foundation — reason — is a degenerate sentiment that easily falls apart; it is seed sown among rocks, which dies lacking the soil in which to germinate.

And because you are Christians and feel the need to believe in something good, serious, and divine, you conform to whatever simply touches your heart, forgetting that in so doing you establish a perpetual struggle between your reason and your emotions, resulting in the

---

[51] Luke, Chapter XIV, verses 16 to 24.

possibility of your weakness, your downfall, and your annihilation.

It is, however, necessary that you reason, seeking the foundations of your faith, and to that end only one reliable means is presented to you: the study of the Holy Gospels in the light of Spiritism.

Do you perhaps fear, upon questioning these sublime and divine truths?

Do you fear, perchance, the anathemas of the Church, which teaches you that outside of it there is no salvation?

But that church is not that of Jesus Christ; that church is that of the priests. It was the one that hurled anathema at the holy men Augustine[52] and Aurelius, Archbishop of Carthage.

It was that church, Christians, which had Clement XIV[53] poisoned because he protested the distortions, the falsehoods, and the reforms undertaken in the Divine Code!

It was that church that burned Girolamo Savonarola[54] at the stake, another protester who paid with his life the great crime of railing against the misuse that the pseudo-successors of Peter then made of the sublime teachings of the Divine Master.

And the holy doctrine of the Lamb of God, the doctrine of love and forgiveness He brought among men to teach them the love of God and of neighbor, pronounced that His representatives on Earth should

---

[52] He was born in 354 in Tagaste, Numidia (Africa). He followed the doctrine of the Manichees for a long time; however, through the efforts of his mother — Saint Monica — he was converted to Christianity and baptized at thirty-two. In 391 he was ordained. In his written discourses he fought the Donatists and Manichees; his major works include: The City of God, Treatises on grace and free will (which earned him the title Doctor of Grace), the Soliloquies, Retractions, Confessions, and a great number of writings against the heretics of his time. Saint Augustine was remarkable for his vast scientific erudition as for his eloquence and great piety; he died in Hippo in 430, during the siege of that city by the Vandals.

[53] Lorenzo Ganganelli — of the Franciscan order; he was born in 1705 and in 1769 succeeded Clement XIII. Gifted with a conciliatory spirit, he lived in good harmony with the courts of Europe. In 1773 he published a brief suppressing the Jesuit order. He died of poisoning in 1774.

[54] A famous Dominican preacher, born in Ferrara (Italy) in 1452. Appointed prior of the Convent of St. Mark in Florence, he became known for his eloquence and great talent, earning the goodwill of the people. He harshly criticized the clergy and the Holy See; and, accused of heresy by Franciscan friars, anathematized by Pope Alexander VI, he was imprisoned and condemned as a heretic. He was burned at the stake on May 23, 1498.

exterminate the Albigenses[55], drowning them in a sea of blood, so that greed and the thirst for temporal power might triumph, all this for God's greater glory and in the name of Jesus!

And are you truly afraid of that church's anathemas, Christians?

Do you not see that the path of light, the holy trail of Our Lord Jesus Christ, protects all who embark upon it from those anathemas, those curses, from all those absurd conventions that find neither support nor justification even in the Old Testament, where harsh laws were demanded by the needs of the age?!

No, Christians, pay no heed to anathemas and excommunications; open the Gospel and in that sublime passage about the adulterous woman[56] you will find Jesus, the Divine Model, who, though not justifying the sin, codifies the holy law of forgiveness and mercy.

Also in the Holy Gospels, in the beautiful parable of the prodigal son[57], you will see that, at any time, the Spirit may atone for its errors, redeem its faults, rising to the realms of light!

Do not be deterred, then, by the anathemas of the Church of Rome; study, while you still possess the light to read! Strengthen your belief, your faith, with reason, in the light of the Gospel!

Come, you who are not bishops nor popes, the poor with no merit other than your desire to be Christians in Christ, come to the feast table to eat the bread of life, devouring with the craving of your poor Spirit that heavenly nourishment which was given to you nineteen centuries ago but which you have still been unable to taste, for men's self-interest kept it hidden from you!

Come learn the gentleness of the Just One, the charity of the Good One, that sublime charity that cannot be found in the so-called church of Jesus, because for that church merely being within it is enough for salvation!

Come and truly understand in spirit and in truth the Lord's Prayer, learning the supreme teaching the Divine Master gave His apostles so

---

[55] Heretics who followed the Manichean doctrines. They inhabited the cities of Albi (which gave them their name), Béziers, Carcassonne, Toulouse, Montauban, Avignon. Pope Alexander III excommunicated them in the Third Council of the Lateran. In 1209, crusaders sent by Pope Innocent III took Béziers, killing 60,000 people, sparing not even the Catholics who were within the city. Innocent III established the Inquisition to uproot the heresy and sent more crusaders against the Albigenses, who were almost completely exterminated.

[56] John, Chapter VIII, verses 1 to 11.

[57] Luke, Chapter XV, verses 1 to 32.

that they, in turn, might give it to all humanity: WITHOUT CHARITY THERE IS NO SALVATION!

FORGIVE MY DEBTS, LORD, AS I FORGIVE MY DEBTORS; this is the simplest and most sublime expression of God's mercy and love!

Here lies the reason why we rise above external formulas of churches, whatever they may be; that is why we deem all that hoard of religious conventions that veer away from the principles established in the Master's doctrine to be devoid of fundamental principles.

And certainly, if a man has charity, if he knows how to forgive his fellow man's debts, why would he need the intervention of a priest or the representative of any other church so that God might also forgive him his sins? If, independent of that spontaneous forgiveness, that pronouncement of the Christian soul, a man still required recourse to this or that place, to the formulas of this or that religion, in order to be forgiven by God, then the creature would be superior to the Creator! Yet that is an absurdity that reason rejects, once it strives to meditate upon the truths which, by the mercy of the Most High, His Divine Son brought to humanity for its salvation.

Thus, in the Lord's Prayer, man finds the true and only formula for his rehabilitation, independent of the intervention of the representative of this or that church; he understands the sublime law of forgiveness and charity, becoming convinced that without it salvation is not possible, no matter how dazzling the glitter, how elaborate the formalities, of any worship to which he might adhere.

And even though we might seek to avoid touching on matters pertaining to the Roman Catholic Apostolic Religion, we cannot, for, intending to speak sincerely and truthfully to Christendom — albeit without the prestige of moral authority — we have set out to address matters that concern its salvation.

The unceasing effort of the Catholic Church to absorb all spiritual and temporal authority within humanity, its eagerness to monopolize divine truth by disguising it according to its own interests, has given rise to constant struggles over many centuries, from which emerge various philosophical associations that, by a natural need of the spirit, seek to reconcile feeling with intellect and reason.

But let us get to the point: is marriage truly a sacrament, as the Catholic Church decrees?

Certainly not, for the principles of a religion that do not find sanction in the Holy Gospels do not belong to the doctrine of Our Lord Jesus Christ.

Now, in the biblical texts, be it the Old or the New Testament, there is not a single expression to justify that! Furthermore, if we look to history, we see that the popes and bishops of the early centuries were married civilly, that is to say, they took on responsibilities as citizens before the civil authority, which in no way impeded the fulfillment of the commitments they also undertook before God, in accordance with their conscience and the sound principles of their religion!

Yet, to those who distorted the holy truths, it seemed necessary to make this mere function of civil authority into a sacrament, so that, through deceitful means, they could heap ridicule and scorn upon the families of representatives of other sects, which they considered offspring of concubinage!

It was necessary, in service to their own interests rather than the interests of the Gospel, to coerce other people's consciences, even if it meant lying through those very conventions, forcing them to pay homage that can be accepted only when it emerges deeply and sincerely from the soul itself, for only then, and only then, does it cease to be hypocrisy and become truth.

And if marriage is just that consent of two souls united by reciprocal feelings of affection and love for the formation of a family, how can one consider it a sacrament?

And if we do so, must we not conclude that the first bishops of the Church committed an offense, given that the same council that considered this social act a sacrament made celibacy a dogma?!

And is celibacy truly an essential condition for someone to be a minister of Jesus on Earth? Surely not, for if that were so — if celibacy were indispensable for the proper functioning of the Church — Peter, the great apostle, who was the head of a family, would not have been given the supreme mission of directing that same Church; the Divine Master would have placed in the world, for such a mission, some man as illustrious as that good fisherman, or He would have seen that Peter was not bound by marital ties.

The Church, however, knows perfectly well the truth; its representatives are aware that the vows of chastity they make are nothing more than mere words! And scandals arise, and humanity, witnessing those deviations (so defined by the Church's own law), asks, seeking some support for its crumbling faith: Lord, where is the truth, where the true religion?

And we reply for the Church: The truth, Christians in Christ, is in the Gospel, and only in the Gospel!

Only in that holy book, in those sublime pages of love and pure light radiating from the sacred bosom of the Divine and Immaculate Son of Mary, shall you learn the true habits of sound morality, forming families so that, beginning in the small circle of your loved ones, to cultivate the flower of that sublime sentiment of love, you may one day come to foster it in the great circle — humanity!

CHAPTER VIII

The true death: the death of the Spirit. — Lazarus's illness; his apparent death and his resurrection. — The scribes and Pharisees decide to put Jesus to death, advised by Caiaphas. — The entrance of the Divine Master into Jerusalem.

Proved the contradiction in which the Roman Catholic Apostolic Church lives, in the face of the principles enshrined in the doctrine of Our Lord Jesus Christ, which formed the subject of the previous chapters, let us follow the steps of the Lord, seeking the knowledge of other truths that further attest to the exaltation of His most pure Spirit, in the performance of the grand mission of guiding miserable humanity—still enslaved by its errors and guilt—along the path of salvation and happiness.

It is not our intention, however, to unfold the entire Gospel before the eyes of Christendom, since in the books of Allan Kardec, in the revelation given to Roustaing, and in the works of Sayão, Júlio César, and so many others, those of good will may find a rich source from which they can freely drink the teachings of Our Divine Master, hitherto veiled by the ill will of some or the malice of others.

Let us, therefore, address the principal points from which we may draw more light for the guidance and understanding of the biblical texts.

Thus, let us open the Gospel, and in Chapter XI of John, let us admire the wonders of faith, seeking to understand in spirit and in truth what happened in the small village of Bethany, where the friend of the Lord lay ill, experiencing an apparent death, to rise again from it, giving glory to God[58].

Lazarus was ill, and his kind sisters, fearful when they observed the ailment's steady advance, which would soon rob them of part of their very soul, sent messengers to Our Lord Jesus Christ, informing Him of the distressful state of their hearts.

And the Lord, as though He were indifferent to Martha's and Mary's sorrow, as though His divine soul did not vibrate with the pure sentiments of charity, remained for a time in the place where He was, not heeding their call, declaring that Lazarus's illness would not result in death, but rather in giving glory to God.

Afterward, addressing His disciples, He said: "Lazarus sleeps," to which they replied: "If he sleeps, Lord, then he will be saved!" Confronted with this statement by His disciples, the evangelist tells us that the Divine Master declared openly: "Lazarus is dead!"

Lazarus dead!

To the disciples, as to all those who were at Martha's and Mary's house, Lazarus was dead, since his face bore the signs of a corpse, and his body showed the inertia of the muscles; to Our Lord Jesus Christ, Lazarus was also dead, indeed, but dead in the Spirit—the true death of which the messengers speak unceasingly to those who devote themselves to the study of the Spiritist Doctrine. This is the death to which the Divine Master always refers in all passages of the Holy Gospels: nothing other than the temporary annihilation in which the Spirit finds itself upon descending to Earth, to enter the tomb of flesh where it must atone for the faults committed.

And it is exactly the contrary that humanity imagines, when it considers that death is life and that life is death.

Behold, therefore, the Divine Master revealing a truth to those who witnessed Lazarus's cataleptic state, a truth consistent with what is perfectly known throughout the spiritual world.

Lazarus could not be dead in that sense as understood by men because, since the Lord's laws are immutable, once the Spirit breaks the bonds that bind it to matter—once the vital fluid that animated the flesh is absorbed into the great whole, at which point the law of decomposition begins—there is absolutely no way for it to return to the corpse and live a material life again.

Could Jesus, perhaps, explain the phenomenon taking place in Lazarus to an uneducated people and, therefore, lacking the necessary elements to understand Him?

---

[58] John, Chapter XI, verses 1 to 57.

If, even today, we cannot find words with which we might express the whole truth, explaining—so as to be understood—all the phenomena that occur before man's very eyes, how could the Divine Master dispel, in those minds, the idea of a miracle?

Lazarus, therefore, suffered from catalepsy, a phenomenon that is now more than well-known, through the study that science has devoted to this pathological condition.

It is certain that, after the sisters of Lazarus gave the greatest testimony of their great faith—the trust and certainty they had that if the Divine Master were present, Lazarus would not die—which prompted the good shepherd of souls to say, "I am the resurrection and the life," when the Lord ordered the stone to be removed from the sepulcher, Martha pointed out that the body already smelled bad, for it had been four days.

This, however, is understandable; it constitutes only a presumption, natural indeed in view of the time elapsed since his apparent death. And even if there was a foul smell, it would have come from the putrid ailment that had afflicted Lazarus before he was overtaken by the cataleptic sleep; his body, however, did not have a corpse-like odor, for real death had not occurred, and thus no decomposition could have taken place.

Christians in Christ, simple and good souls who, despite the great shipwreck of Peter's boat, can still glimpse on the horizon the white sail that seeks the path to the salvation of your Spirit! Simple and good souls who, in the black night that closes over the expanse of your wretched planet, can still behold the luminous torch which, like the Magi's star, guides you to the hut of the Redeemer of the world: strengthen within yourselves the sentiments of Martha and Mary; let the withered flower of hope blossom in your Spirits, awaiting the gentle dew that, from the heights of light, flows out of the bosom of the Blessed Master upon its petals!

Have confidence, like these humble women, that where Jesus is, there is resurrection and life; consider yourselves as Lazarus, who lies within your tombs of flesh, with that heavy stone of Rome's Church upon you, crushing your hearts!

Believe and hope in Our Lord Jesus Christ, who comes to bring you the rising up, the lifting of your soul torn by the pain caused by the thorns and brambles strewn across the road of your earthly pilgrimage!

And yet, that extraordinary event, deemed a miracle and performed by the Divine Master upon Lazarus, was the immediate cause of the Lord's condemnation.

When this news spread throughout Judea, the people came in great numbers to seek out that Spirit who, in addition to making the paralyzed walk and giving sight to the blind, raised the dead; thus, astonished—some thirsting for the wondrous, others filled with regret—they all came to prostrate themselves at the Lord's feet, pleading for forgiveness of their sins!

At a distance, in the distance of pride and selfishness, stood the scribes and Pharisees, murmuring against the Divine Lamb, who attracted to Himself the crowd that surrounded Him, eager for the purest light that shone in His divine and serene countenance.

And fearing that He might be proclaimed king, they said among themselves: "We, who hold the official positions granted to us by Caesar's Rome—we, who have interests to protect—should we allow this absorption of our power?

"Will Rome not send its armies once again to subjugate us, unsatisfied with the gold tribute we already pay Caesar?"

So they conspired, when Caiaphas, the pontiff that year, giving his considered opinion, declared that it was necessary for that man to die so that the nation might be saved! Poor man that he was—he did not understand that that great Spirit had to depart from the surface of the Earth not for the salvation of a single people, but for the salvation of all humanity!

Thus the dark plan was decided, and they awaited only the opportunity to put the Divine Master to death. However, as the hour had not yet come for the spirit of darkness to have full freedom to act with all the ferocity of those tiger-like hearts, Jesus sought a small retreat, where He remained for a few days with His disciples, away from the Jews.

Six days before the festivities, the Beloved Disciple tells us, the Lord prepared to depart toward the Daughter of Zion, where He was to eat the Passover with His disciples. Hardly had this news spread among the people than they all prepared to lead the Son of Mary to the holy city in triumph.

And among the good, humble people, a deep and genuine emotion arose that they were about to pay the greatest and final tributes to which the most loving, the purest of Spirits—descended to Earth—had a right. And the road was covered with palms and flowers; cloaks were thrown onto the path along which He was to pass, riding the humble beast used by the poor, the Divine Redeemer, acclaimed by the old, the young, and the children, who cried: "HOSANNA TO THE

ONE WHO COMES IN THE NAME OF THE LORD!⁵⁹"

And these rapturous hymns of glory drowned out the shouts of so many others who cried: "Death, death to the Son of Mary!"

Frightened, some of the Pharisees pleaded with the Divine Master to silence the crowds glorifying Him, to which the Gentle Lamb replied: "I assure you that, if they keep silent, the very stones of the road will cry out!"

And indeed, perhaps the stones of the road were less hardened than were those hearts, which longed for silence while plotting the perpetration of an abominable crime!

Yet, in spite of it all, the Divine Master entered Jerusalem, receiving from the people the final honors they would pay Him on Earth, on His way to Calvary!

Let us follow Him, Christians in Christ; let us witness His supper, there seeking yet other examples of humility and love from the Divine Lamb, toward His disciples and toward all humanity!

---

[59] Mathews, Chapter XXI, verses 1 to 11. Mark, Chapter XI, verses 1 to 11. Luke, Chapter XIX, verses 29 to 40. John, Chapter XII, verses 12 to 15.

CHAPTER IX

The Paschal Supper. — The Eucharist. — Jesus washes the feet of His disciples. — Prediction of Judas's betrayal. — The many mansions in the Father's House. — The Consoler. — Jesus predicts that Peter will deny Him three times[60].

The resurrection of Lazarus filled the cup with the dregs of the most heinous passions, which, overflowing, would bring about the tremendous crime against the gentle son of Mary — the Redeemer of men!

Foreseeing the events that were about to take place, the Divine Master wishes, for the last time, to commemorate the Passover with His disciples; with the terrible moment of anguish approaching, after which He was to ascend to the Father, He seeks, in the solemnity of this ceremony that was taking place close to His death, to make His testament, sharing with His beloved disciples the great treasures of His love, even with the ungrateful one who, driven by ambition, would deliver Him into the hands of His executioners!

And of all His belongings—His peace, His love, His humility—He disposed, like a most loving father, showing His disciples the luminous path that should lead them to conquer the supreme truth, there in those many mansions of His Father's house, to which He was going before them, to prepare them places.

Yet from all this solemnity, from everything that happened on that terrible night of anguish, two extraordinary facts took place, to which we call the attention of Christendom, seeking to explain them, as far as

---

[60] Matthew, Chapter XXVI, verses 17 to 35. Mark, Chapter XIV, verses e12 to 31. Luke, Chapter XXII, verses 7 to 34. John, Chapter XIII.

our understanding allows and as far as it is granted to us by the sovereign grace of the Lord!

Seated at the table, full of sadness, for His divine Spirit foresaw the dreadful drama being woven in the shadows against Him, the Lord takes the bread and, offering it to His disciples, says to them: "Eat; this is My body;" and, presenting them the cup of wine, on which an artist had engraved the sacrifice of Isaac, He further says: "Drink; this is My blood![61]"

But can we, interpreting literally the words of the Divine Master, consider the bread and the wine the body and the blood of Our Lord Jesus Christ?

Or do these expressions conceal a truth that could not be understood in those times?

And regarding this passage, might there not have been an omission of some word on the part of the evangelists?

Yes, certainly; that omission occurred, I affirm to you, Christians in Christ. Jesus, offering the bread and wine to His disciples, said to them: "Eat; this is the symbol of My body; drink; this is the symbol of My blood!"

And thus, materially, Jesus had spoken a truth, for, as I had occasion to tell you in Chapter I of this humble work, His body, apparently human, was composed precisely of the constitutive fluids of these two elements of life; spiritually, He still spoke truth, for in this solemn Passover celebration the Lord represented the Meek Lamb who, for the salvation of all humanity, was to be sacrificed!

"Eat of the bread, drink of the wine, symbols of the constitution of My body, which you believe to be like yours, and do this, every year, in memory of My name!"

And this merely means: just as the Jews gathered every year in family to celebrate the day when they passed from the lands of captivity to those of freedom, so too should the disciples of Jesus gather to commemorate the day of His anguish, which is also the day on which, by His divine word, He lifted them from the shadows of death to the dawn of life!

However, men, in their eagerness to materialize everything, created, from the sublimity of that ceremony, a sacrament to which they gave the name of the Eucharist!

But, my God, must we indeed break the silence of the tomb in order

---

[61] Matthew, Chapter XXVI, verses 26 to 28. Mark, Chapter XIV, verses 22 to 24. Luke, Chapter XXII, verses 19 and 20.

to tell them how absurd is this creation of the Catholic Church, which degrades the memory of the greatest of the Spirits who have come down to Earth? Must we still tell you how repugnant it is to the believer's soul, this act by which a host is consecrated, symbolizing the fluidic body of the Divine Lamb, to be ingested and then eliminated by the human organism, in obedience to the inescapable law of nutritional processes?

What subterfuges of language, what skill must be employed to justify such an affront?

For they do not understand that the words of Jesus were and are spirit and life, and that, though veiled by the letter, they were meant to offer the disciples, as well as all humanity, the true teachings that, bringing solutions to the great problems of life, are entirely independent of material formulas, which serve no purpose and hold no value, because, as I have often told you, they find no foundation in the Holy Gospels!

And, in the nineteenth century, when the promised Consoler knocks at our door, we still see the priest take the emblematic body of Our Lord Jesus Christ and ingest it in front of the ignorant multitude, whom he tries to convince that this ceremony alone suffices to remit sins!

Christians in Christ, the true successors of Peter, I say to you, they never, not even in a dream, not even for a moment, imagined commemorating this solemn event of Passover believing they were imbibing in the bread and wine the body and blood of our Divine Redeemer! They never did it, because they never strayed from the righteous path of justice and mercy; therefore, they always had in their souls sufficient light to understand, in spirit and life, the words of the Beloved Master, which revealed to them the holy doctrine of love and peace they were charged to spread upon the Earth!

And while such wrongs are committed in the name of the Gospel, that very memorable night we find the Meek Lamb, God's representative on Earth, on His knees before His disciples, washing their feet and drying them with the towel with which He had girded Himself, having risen from the table! And this was the greatest example of humility that the Divine Master gave them so they might, by following it, fulfill the high mission of tending His flock.

"You call Me Master and Lord, and you say well, for that is what I am! But if, being your master and your lord, I wash your feet, what then should you do to one another? Be humble; love one another as I love you and as the Father loves you, and only thus will you be recognized as My true disciples.⁶²"

Behold the sublime words of the Envoy of God, who came down to Earth to show sorrowful humanity, still enslaved by its own passions, the path of light that should lead it, redeemed and cleansed of sin, to the feet of the Creator!

And yet there exists on Earth a man, a successor of Peter, who, reading this grand passage of the Gospel—the supreme lesson of Christian humility—interprets it and puts it into practice by sitting upon a sumptuous chair, where he watches the pilgrims, from all over the world, pass by reverently to kiss his feet!

And thus is the Gospel of Our Lord Jesus Christ interpreted!

I know, Christians in Christ, that deep sorrows will wound your souls as you read these pages I now dictate; I see that a world of doubts crowds your Spirit, overwhelming you, causing you to falter, shaking your faith, since, accustomed to such practices, you had already set yourselves to accept all these absurdities as truth!

And if I came only to disturb the serenity of your spirit, without being able at once to provide a palliative, a balm for your despair arising from the crumbling of beliefs in what had, until then, been your truth, I would certainly be a wicked person. But if I speak to you in this way, it is because among you already is found the PROMISED CONSOLER—THE SPIRITIST DOCTRINE—a lavish source of all the truths that must replace the worm-eaten structure of your beliefs, showing you the secure route, the narrow gate: the heart, the soul of the Divine Master, Who, forgiving your mistakes, covers you with His divine mantle of love, leading you to supreme happiness!

"I am the vine, and My Father is the husbandman," says the Divine Lamb!

We, Christians, are the branches that, remaining in the divine trunk—our Divine Master—must bear the fruits that will attest to the benefit of the teachings that, so many centuries ago, God's mercy offered us.

And if it is certain that the wickedness of men seeks to corrupt your sap, behold the celestial dew bathing your soul, so that you may bring forth the fruits expected of you. And certainly you will succeed, Christians in Christ, if you study the Good News, the consoling doctrine that, for love of men, the Lord has once again sent to Earth!

And let not your mistakes be a cause for discouragement; remember that the Divine Jesus, at the Paschal Supper table, also gave Judas, who

---

⁶² John, Chapter XIII, verses 4 to 15.

was to betray Him, the bread and wine He had shared with all His disciples; remember that He knelt at his feet as well, to wash them! And from the height of the cross, invoking forgiveness for all who hated Him, He extends His infinite love, His divine mercy, to all those who seek Him in the wings of fervent prayer, guiding them along the luminous path that must lead them, pure and cleansed of the stains of sin, to the feet of His and our Creator and Father!

Without lingering, however, on this sublime passage from the Holy Gospels—in which Jesus Christ, our Divine Master, the greatest Spirit ever to come down to Earth, is most exalted as He humbles Himself before men—let us follow the narrative of the Beloved Disciple, seeking new teachings, which, giving us courage, will embolden us in the new crusade in which we engage, for the restoration of evangelical truths.

And since we cannot, under any circumstance, take at face value everything contained in the Gospels, it is crucial that we strive, interpreting in spirit and life the sublime teachings, to properly understand the Good News of Our Lord Jesus Christ.

The Beloved Disciple[63] tells us that after the Lord gave Judas the dipped bread, Satan entered into him, who on Earth would lead him to the dark betrayal of the Divine Master. If we take literally the evangelist's words, we fall into the absurd notion that Our Lord Jesus Christ was handing Judas over to the spirit of darkness in the food He offered him at the Paschal Supper table.

But these words—"Satan entered into him"—are figurative and merely signify that, in Judas's spirit, the idea of crime had begun to germinate and now took hold as a resolution.

It was time for the prophecies to be fulfilled; it was necessary that the Meek Lamb was led to sacrifice for the redemption of men!

And if you leaf through the Gospels, Christians in Christ, you will find numerous passages where our Divine Master is pursued by the crowds who attempt to take His life, yet He disappears from their sight, for His time had not yet come, which abundantly proves that the body cloaking Him was of a fluidic nature.

The prince of this world—that is, evil—could not yet take hold of those who were to put the Beloved Lamb to death; an atmosphere of light surrounded Him, into which the wicked—those who hated Jesus and His dear disciples charged with spreading over Earth the holy doctrine of love and forgiveness He had preached—could not

---

[63] John, Chapter XIII, verses 26 and 27.

penetrate.

Once the divine banquet was over, the Lord having made His testament—that is, having given His disciples the instructions necessary for them to fulfill on Earth the holy mission with which He had entrusted them—this atmosphere of light is dispelled by an act of His divine will, and thus begins the reign of darkness; and, fully unrestrained, the perfidious and ungrateful act upon those in whom they find the necessary elements for the sacrifice of the Divine Redeemer!

The evangelists, despite the elevation of their Spirits and the lofty ministry with which they were invested, could not comprehend, in spirit and truth, all the teachings of the Beloved Master; thus, upon seeing Judas, after receiving the dipped bread, disappear from the banquet room transformed, they deduced that Satan had taken possession of him at the very moment he received the food.

And yet, at that moment, the prophecy of the Meek Lamb was being fulfilled; for when His dear disciples asked, He showed them the traitor; and the adversaries of Jesus, adversaries of His doctrine of salvation, stepped fully into their evil influence, Judas—by his ambition for gold and power—being chosen to deliver into the hands of the scribes and Pharisees the gentle and beloved Son of Mary!

The Divine Master could not reveal the entire truth of His teachings to His disciples; He Himself said it, according to what we read in John, Chapter XVI, verse 12: "I have yet many things to say unto you, but ye cannot bear them now."

Thus, when speaking of the many mansions in His Father's House[64], it is clear that to His disciples, simple and ignorant though they were—albeit filled with love, light, and faith—He could by no means explain to them that these many mansions comprising the Father's House, which is the Universe, were nothing more, as we now know, than those millions of planets populating space, where Spirits strive to progress, fulfilling their missions according to their degree of moral and intellectual advancement, since the ascending hierarchy of these worlds relates directly to the hierarchy of the Spirits that inhabit them.

They therefore could not bear the unfolding of all His divine teachings, but the time would come—and it has already arrived—when the Good News, the essence of the truths taught by the Meek Lamb, shall be understood by His disciples and by all humanity. This is found

---

[64] John, Chapter XIV, verse 2.

in John, Chapter XIV, verse 26, where the Divine Master declares that the Consoler shall come, which is the Holy Spirit—that is, the legion of the Lord's envoys—to teach all things, reminding us of all that He had said.

The Consoler is Spiritism; through it, the teachings of Jesus shall be understood in spirit and truth, and those who sincerely believe in Our Lord Jesus Christ, placing themselves beneath His holy banner, shall have abundant light to follow the luminous trail that leads the creature to the bosom of its Creator and Father.

But let us return to the evangelist's account.

Having made His testament, declaring to His disciples His intention to withdraw from Earth to a place where they could not yet follow Him, Peter, not understanding His Divine Master's words, asks why he cannot follow, since he is determined to surrender both soul and life for Him.

To that question, the Lord replies, riveting the attention of the fervently faithful apostle, and of the other disciples, so He might firmly impress upon their spirits His prediction: "Wilt thou lay down thy life for My sake? Verily, verily, I say unto thee, the cock shall not crow till thou hast denied Me thrice![65]"

Peter was thus also chosen by the spirits of darkness to cause scandal to the Lord; they intended to sift him likewise, and perhaps they would have succeeded, weakened by the flesh that enveloped him, had the Divine Master not interceded for the old fisherman to whom He had entrusted the leadership of His Church on Earth.

This shows, Christians in Christ, how vigilant we must be in the world, especially when we have resolved to give our life and soul for our Master and Lord.

And, though it may seem paradoxical, it is the truth!

The more a Spirit seeks to free itself from the vices and passions that degrade it, the more it is beset by the wretched, striving to dissuade it from its good intentions.

Peter was a man: his Spirit was clothed in flesh which, as the Divine Lord so often said, is weak; and although he ardently wished never to abandon his dear friend for a single moment, strange influences assailed him and, unable to corrupt the depths of his soul—already touched by the sacred breath of his Divine Master—they terrify him, thus accomplishing their goal of making him publicly deny Our Lord

---

[65] John, Chapter XIII, verse 38. Luke, Chapter XXII, verse 34. Mark, Chapter XIV, verse 30. Matthew, Chapter XXVI, verse 34.

Jesus Christ. Hence, the scandal they so desired was realized.

In this manner, foreseeing what lay ahead, the Meek Lamb predicted that he would deny Him three times.

Continuing his account, the evangelist says that after giving His final instructions to His disciples, the Lord went out with them to the other side of the brook Cedron, where there was a garden, in which He sought seclusion.

This shall be the subject of the following chapter.

CHAPTER X

The Kiss of Betrayal. — Peter strikes Malchus's ear. — The three denials of the Apostle of Faith. — Pilate's efforts to free the Divine Lord. — Judas's repentance. — Words of the Gentle Lamb to the daughters of Jerusalem. — Calvary. — Jesus's words to the Most Holy Virgin and to the Beloved Disciple. — The Divine Master's final words. — Nicodemus and Joseph of Arimathea lay the body of Jesus in the tomb.

The Garden of Olives, the pleasant spot so often sought by the Lord for the repose of His humble disciples and companions, and where, away from the large crowds, He would reveal to them the truths of life beyond the grave, comforting their souls during those sweet moments when the cups of the roses would open up as though they, too, were speaking in the mysterious language of perfumes, this Garden of Olives was the place chosen for the great scandal that still today troubles and fills Christian hearts with dread!

His friends and disciples, saddened by the last words the Beloved Master had spoken to them, lay down on the grass and, weary, fall asleep. Jesus, the evangelists recount[66], moving a little distance away from them, falls to His knees on the ground and, in a gentle plea, asks the Father to turn away from Him the cup of His harsh agonies, carrying out, however, His divine will.

And certainly, the Divine Lamb prayed at that moment, yet the anointed prayer that issued from His lips reached the feet of the Creator with supplications for His cruel tormentors. His spotless Spirit

---

[66] Matthew, Chapter XXVI, verses 36 to 39. Mark, Chapter XIV, verses 32 to 36. Luke, Chapter XXII, verses 39 to 42.

did not suffer that faltering which troubles those who approach death; indeed there was, in His soul, sorrow and agony, but sorrow at the ingratitude of men, agony inspired by the vision of the future, which assured Him how much, in His name and for His holy doctrine, those careless ones who allowed themselves to fall asleep on the grass would suffer.

And if, to spare His dear companions the bitter torments that awaited them, it was necessary for the cup to be turned away from His divine lips, Jesus asked the Father that it be so, yet, at the same time, that His most holy will should always and ever prevail.

Having made this plea, the Lord approaches His beloved companions, awakens them, warning them that they must stay vigilant, for the prince of this world, that is, the legion of hatred, envy, and falsehood, was coming to seize them.

Barely has the Lord finished advising them when the cohort of His fierce enemies appears.

Judas, at the front, so as to identify Him readily, goes up to Him, giving Him the kiss of betrayal. The Divine Master gazes compassionately at the ungrateful disciple and, turning to those around him, asks: "Whom do you seek?" — "Jesus of Nazareth," they answer. — "I am He," says the Divine Lamb; and at these words, the scribes and Pharisees fall to the ground.

This event clearly demonstrates to Christendom the power of Our Lord Jesus Christ. When the Lord declares that He is truly the Righteous One Forechosen, His sovereign Spirit stands revealed in all His greatness, His most pure light radiates, the garden is illuminated, and the soldiers of the cohort tumble to the earth, confounded.

But, as His hour had come, Jesus hides Himself once more, takes on the form of a man of this world, concentrates that divine radiance within His breast, and surrenders Himself as a captive. Peter, however, takes up the sword and strikes one of the soldiers of the cohort[67]!

And why, you will certainly ask, why does a disciple of Our Lord Jesus Christ arm himself against the enemies of his Master?

— Simply because, taking literally the advice given to him a few moments earlier, he thought he should resort to this instrument of death to defend himself and his friends!

And yet the counsel of the Divine Lamb was merely symbolic, which the humble fisherman was unable to understand.

---

[67] John, Chapter XVIII, verses 1 to 11. Luke, Chapter XXII, verses 47 to 51. Mark, Chapter XIV, verses 43 to 47. Matthew, Chapter XXVI, verses 47 to 52.

— "When I sent you out without purse and without a traveling bag," the Divine Master asks His disciples, "did you lack anything? So now I say to you: take a purse and a traveling bag, and let the one who has none sell his cloak and buy a sword!"

And would a sword, by any chance, make up for the lack of a purse? Certainly not.

Jesus had spoken symbolically to His disciples; He was alluding to the one and only true sword the Christian can wield: the sword of faith, the only one he should use so that he not lack nourishment for the body or for the Spirit—courage in the struggle that was about to be waged between truth and error, between light and darkness!

Thus He was saying: while you were with Me, you lacked nothing, because My power supplied everything; now, however, I go to the Father and leave you orphans in this world. You must therefore equip yourselves with that powerful means of combat—the sanctifying faith, the faith that has the unconquerable strength for all the undertakings of the spirit.

Still, despite the illusion of that great Apostle of Faith, it was fitting that the event should unfold, for it held a lesson for the future.

Otherwise, it would be illogical that Jesus, who had advised His disciples to take a sword, would tell Peter moments later, as the biblical texts report: "Put your sword away, for all who take up the sword shall die by the sword."

Those words of the Divine Master were a clear condemnation of religious wars that would later arise, as history tells us, in which the human heart has been drowned in a sea of blood, in the name of the Divine Lamb.

They were a warning to all those who, in the future, would present themselves as the continuers of His holy work and who, indifferent to the truths contained in His Good News, replaced the cross with the blade, spreading out over the surface of the Earth under the pretense of conversion so as to sow thorns and briars in the Lord's field, until they stifled the tender plants that would flourish anew through sanctified effort, through the evangelical labor of His true disciples.

Therefore, Jesus did not advise Peter to take up arms against the opponents of His doctrine, nor did He authorize the pseudo-Christians to gain converts at the cost of their brothers' blood.

And alongside that lesson, He gives His disciples an even greater one, healing Malchus's ear, thus practicing charity toward His persecutor.

Then, without further resistance, He surrenders and walks toward the house of His judges. The disciples, terrified by all these events of which they were witnesses, flee; Peter, however, who had resolved not to abandon his dear Friend, offering for Him even his own life, follows the ignorant throng and, managing to enter the courtyard of the palace of the Lord's judge, sits down on a stone, waiting calmly for the outcome of the trial.

A servant girl approaches him, asking if he, too, belonged to the Lord's followers; the Apostle, afraid that his answer might influence his Divine Master's condemnation in some way, denies it. Another person then asks him the same question, and Peter denies it a second time. A third, noticing him and denouncing him as the one who, armed with a sword, had wounded one of the law's servants, forces him to deny it a third time, and immediately afterward, the rooster crows.

So is fulfilled the prophecy of the Divine Master, who, through the bars of Caiaphas's house, casts a compassionate glance at the great Apostle[68].

Peter weeps bitterly, realizing he did not know how to stand firm then with the true sword to declare the truth, for the truth is always proclaimed when one has faith, when one holds true belief, because the truth is God, the truth is Jesus!

Indoors, the Divine Lamb was being judged, accused of monstrous crimes; for those people, love and charity were an insult, while compassion and mercy were a cry of sedition that could topple Caesar's throne!

And, among the mob surrounding them, they sought, with all their might, someone who would come forward, clearly and decisively, to accuse the Divine Master. Failing to find anyone, the leaders of Judea sent the pitiable captive from one to another until one of them might have the cunning to discover a crime that would take Him to the cross!

And the crime was found: Jesus had spoken the most scandalous phrase that could be heard in Palestine. He had confessed, in public and before the very judge, that He was the Son of God!

All Pilate's efforts to deliver the gentle son of Mary from that people's tiger-like rage were in vain! He offered them the freedom of the Divine Lamb, as part of the act of clemency customary during the Passover celebration, but the scribes and Pharisees, the fanatical and ferocious crowd, chose the freedom of a criminal, demanding the crucifixion of Our Lord Jesus Christ.

---

[68] Matthew, Chapter XXVI, verses 69 to 75. Mark, Chapter XIV, verses 66 to 72. Luke, Chapter XXII, verses 55 to 62. John, Chapter XVIII, verses 15 to 18. John, Chapter XVIII, verses 25 to 27.

Cowardly, and for personal advancement, Pilate has Him dressed in the garment of the condemned, and, washing his hands before the crowd, exclaims: "I am innocent of the blood of this just Man," and, rendering his sentence, hands Him over to the soldiers' brutality.

They, mocking Him—since they believed Him ambitious for a throne—dress Him in purple, place on His head a crown of thorns, and in His right hand a green reed plucked from the marshes of Palestine. Thus, a plaything for the populace, the Lord proceeds, while the nefarious work of the Spirit of darkness is completed[69]!

And Judas, his conscience now free, seized with remorse, hastens to return the thirty coins to those who had purchased his devotion and the affections of his Divine Master.

It is too late; Jesus has already received His death sentence. The traitor, panic-stricken, throws at the feet of the Pharisees and scribes that money that burns his hands and seeks to vanish from the face of the Earth, committing yet another crime: suicide.

The priests take that money, which, being blood money, could not be placed in the donation chest, and decide to use it to buy the potter's field, which they set aside as a cemetery for foreigners. That field came to be called "Field of Blood," and so that money, with which a conscience had been corrupted in order to crucify a just Man, still ended up being used for a charitable deed!

And the Lord kept walking; and the people—women, children, and the elderly—were weeping, exclaiming aloud: "If this happens to the green wood, what will happen to the dry?!"

And the little children, His sweet friends who had so often rested on His knees, receiving His divine affection, looked at Him in amazement, unable to understand why He was being led away from their loving hearts!

And the Divine Master, casting a compassionate glance upon the crowd following Him, says: "Daughters of Jerusalem, do not weep for Me; weep for yourselves, for the time will come when people will say: 'Blessed is she whose breasts none have suckled; blessed the barren whose wombs have borne no children!'"

As the divine prophet, He foresaw the horrors of civil war that would one day erupt among the Jews over disagreements in religious practices, which He had so ardently fought against at the cost of His most bitter martyrdom! He saw that Holy City so recently crowned

---

[69] John, Chapter XVIII, verses 28 to 40. John, Chapter XIX, verses 1 to 19. Matthew, Chapter XXVII, verses 1 to 37. Mark, Chapter XV, verses 1 to 26. Luke, Chapter XXIII, verses 1 to 38.

with triumphs and glories—whence He had just come—struck down by sword and fire. It was as though He was already witnessing that dreadful carnage that would befall Jerusalem's children, subjugated by Rome's mighty armies yet again, seeking by force to dominate all of Palestine. In those days of horror, when mothers, driven to desperation by hunger, would devour their own children, and all the soul's affections lay mute in the human heart, overshadowed by the urge for survival, the Divine Master walked on in His shameful journey to Calvary and, seeing on the faces of those around Him—pale from shock at His bitter martyrdom—the tears flowing, He told them: "Do not weep for Me, children of Jerusalem; weep for yourselves and for your offspring!"

Seventy years later, the temple where the Most Loving Lamb had so many times entered to show the people the loftiness of His doctrine of salvation lay in ruins; the sacred books were taken to pagan Rome, a mockery to the ignorant crowds!

The true believers—those who had received the seed in good soil— were imprisoned, some enslaved, others thrown to wild beasts, as entertainment for the raging throng!

And it was from the shadows of His harsh martyrdom that the Lord, beholding that hateful tableau, asked the poor women not to lament Him, for He was returning to the palace of His Exalted Father, while they and future generations would remain until the hour of the destruction of the Holy City should come!

Bent beneath the weight of the beam, amid the sobbing and groans of His beloved companions, Jesus proceeds toward the throne of Redemption, toward the altar of the world—the Golgotha! And more than once, yielding to its enormous burden, His divine face fell to the ground; the hour of His great sacrifice approached slowly!

It was then that the scribes and Pharisees, not out of pity but because night was drawing near, sought someone to help the Lord carry His cross. Simon of Cyrene, stepping out from the crowd, presented himself, and thus the Lord was able to reach the dark mount of Calvary where He would suffer a disgraceful death. There, filled with heavenly resignation, her most gentle motherly feelings wounded, stood the grief-stricken Holy Virgin with the Beloved Disciple, awaiting her poor, ill-fated Son, who, as she believed, was going to His death because He had loved so greatly!

And hatred and envy still were not satisfied with the Redeemer of the World's crucifixion! They also wanted shame and granted it, placing two thieves at His side!

It was necessary for the people to think He was no different from common criminals; and so, to prove that the Divine Lamb was nothing more than an impostor and that all His wondrous works were merely a product of His disciples' diseased imaginations, they aimed insults at Him, shouting for Him to perform one more miracle by coming down from the cross, putting His torturers to shame!

And to their invectives and jeers, the gentle Nazarene replied: "FATHER, FORGIVE THEM, FOR THEY KNOW NOT WHAT THEY DO!"

Those words were yet another example of love and resignation that the Divine Master bequeathed to the world! In His agonies, in His deepest suffering, not a single word of reproach escapes His lips!

And upon the frenzied crowd around Him, He casts a compassionate look—pure, divine light which, like the sun of all suns, before it sinks in the west, spreads its shining rays over the heads of His fierce and sullen enemies!

After tasting the dregs of the cup, symbol of His bitter ordeals, the Lord turns to the Holy Virgin and, with a glance at the Beloved Disciple, exclaims: "Woman, behold your son!"

In so doing, once again, under the veil of the letter, He teaches humanity that the anguished Virgin before Him, His companion in tribulation, had not given Him being as His mother, that she was not so, yet that her grief and her tears were none the less, for if there were no mother and son there, there were two souls linked by the same love that had created them, the same feeling—true and pure love known only in heaven[70]!

And revelry reigned atop Calvary; sated with cruelty, hearts turned beastly. They drank and reveled, trying to drown out the sorrowful echo of His groans in the wild cries of that disgraceful bacchanal.

And to fulfill the prophecies, they cast lots for the Lord's tunic until, at the sixth hour, after all had been accomplished, Jesus let out a great cry to call the crowd's attention, saying: "IT IS FINISHED! INTO YOUR HANDS, LORD, I COMMEND MY SPIRIT!"

Before that, having promised the so-called good thief in the Gospel's words that he would be with Him in paradise, that man, seeing the Lord's head drop, uttered the words which were ascribed to Jesus: *"Ely, Ely, lamma sabachtani!"*—'Lord, Lord, why have You forsaken me?!"

Such was the confusion, such the appalling tragedy, such the

---

[70] John, Chapter XIX, verses 26 and 27.

horrifying scene, that the onlookers, distraught, believed that these words of anguish and despair had come from the Divine Lamb's own lips!

But it was not so, nor could it be: Jesus, the Righteous One forechosen, whose Spirit was forever at the feet of His glorious Father; Jesus, who had braved all mankind's fury and wickedness, could not, at that supreme moment, yield to those weaknesses that afflict only sinful souls.

No, Christians in Christ, I affirm to you, as a Spirit and by the truth I receive from my superiors, the elevated Spirits who guide me in this work: The words uttered by Jesus in His final moments were these, and these alone: "IT IS FINISHED! INTO YOUR HANDS, LORD, I COMMEND MY SPIRIT!"

Nicodemus and Joseph of Arimathea, disciples of Our Lord Jesus Christ, though hidden for fear of the Jews, obtained Pilate's permission to remove the Lord's body from the cross, which they did. After wrapping it in a shroud and anointing it with the sweetest perfumes, they laid it in a new tomb located near the place where the Divine Master had been crucified.

But the scribes and Pharisees, fearing that the disciples would come by night to steal their Master's body in order to make His anticipated resurrection seem real, also asked Pilate for a guard to watch the tomb—a large guard that could keep vigil in shifts, thus ensuring complete security[71].

How the Lord rose again and the events that took place following His resurrection will be the subject of our next and final chapter.

---

[71] John, Chapter XIX, verses 28 to 42. Luke, Chapter XXIII, verses 39 to 56. Mark, Chapter XV, verses 27 to 47. Matthew, Chapter XXVII, verses 38 to 66.

CHAPTER XI

Visit of the devout women to the holy sepulcher. — Apparition of the Divine Master to Mary Magdalene. — Magdalene, by the Lord's command, informs the disciples of His resurrection. — Apparition of the Divine Master to His disciples. — Thomas's unbelief. — Jesus manifests Himself once more to His disciples, in Thomas's presence. — Words of the Divine Lord to the Apostle of Faith. — The Lord's Ascension — The Consoler among humankind — The Spiritist Doctrine.

In the midst of applause and revelry, the tragedy of Calvary had come to an end.

The silent night descended from the sidereal expanse, enshrouding the soil of Palestine, so many times traversed by the Gentle Lamb, who, in His passage, had left deep furrows of boundless love.

In the foliage of the trees, the gentle birds sought their sheltered nests and, as if sharing in the sorrow of those kind souls, they chirped tender laments of longing.

Far away, still filled with amazement at the dark crime of the cross, the Lord's friends gathered together to recall His holy teachings, seeking in one another's fraternal encouragement the strength needed to carry the Beloved Master's Good News to distant lands.

And as soon as night once again draped the face of the earth with the same mantle, with the first fires of dawn arising in the eastern skies, there they came, braving the insults and mockery of the praetorian guard, the good women, the daughters of Jerusalem, bearing fresh roses and intoxicating balms to fill the holy sepulcher with perfumes; and, full of devotion, they prayed, while copious tears bathed their faces, a sorrowful weeping that perhaps summed up all that immense pain rooted in the heart of the purest, holiest of women — the Immaculate Virgin Mother[72]!

One day, however, the first day of the week, when, at daybreak, the devout women came, as on other days, bringing flowers and perfumes to the sacred dead, they were amazed to find the stone rolled away from the sepulcher and, in the emptiness of the tomb, neatly folded, the shroud and vestments of Him who had been condemned by humankind.

Struck by the suspicion that the Lord's tomb had been profaned, so as to prevent that visit which had become unwelcome to those men, they rushed to inform the Lamb's disciples of all they had witnessed.

Magdalene sought Peter, to whom she conveyed the sad news; but he did not believe her. He went with her and with the Beloved Disciple to the sepulcher, where he verified the truth of the penitent woman's words. He then left with John and told their companions of that extraordinary event.

Mary, however, remained weeping by the tomb, when two Spirits, becoming visible to her, asked her the reason for her tears.

"They have taken my Lord," the sorrowful one replied, whereupon one of the divine guardians of the sepulcher said to her: "Seek Him farther on!"

Hearing these words, Mary moved a few steps away and, astonished, saw before her a radiant Spirit who also asked her about her sorrow.

Mary gave Him the same reply, and then that Spirit, taking on the form of the Divine Lamb, uttered her name; filled with joy, the repentant woman ran to cover with kisses the feet of her Divine Master.

Jesus, however, did not allow it, saying to her: "Do not touch Me, for I have not yet ascended to My Father!"

The Divine Master, as all who study the New Revelation know, immediately after the fulfillment of His sacrifice, which was exposed to the fury of the Pharisees and scribes, and to the zeal and reverence of the good, no longer retained that apparent body with which He had presented Himself to the world to carry out His sacred mission. As soon as that body was placed in the tomb and sealed with the heavy stone closing the sepulcher, Jesus, by the power of His divine will, drew it up into space, restoring its condition, which had always been purely

---

[72] Matthew, Chapter XXVIII, verses 1 to 10. Mark, Chapter XVI, verses 1 to 16. Luke, Chapter XXIV, verses 1 to 40. John, Chapter XX, verses 1 to 23.

fluidic.

That other body, however, seen by Magdalene, was the perispirit of the Divine Master, which she could not touch because she would have found nothing but emptiness. And that was why Our Lord Jesus Christ, who had so many times allowed the repentant woman's expressions of love, letting her kiss His feet and hands, bathing them with her abundant tears and drying them with her hair, in that moment, under the pretext that He had not yet ascended to the Father, would not let her touch Him.

"Go," the Lord said to her, "tell My disciples that I have risen from the dead." And Magdalene eagerly ran to bring them the good news.

They, however, did not believe her, for they did not well remember what the Scriptures said, affirming that on the third day the Savior of the world had to rise again.

And at dusk that same day, the Lord's friends were together behind closed doors, for fear of the Jews, in the blessed companionship of prayer and longing, when, in their midst, the Divine Master appeared. What followed at that moment cannot be expressed in words!

The Lord opened their understanding; the veil that obscured the grandeur of Our Lord Jesus Christ's mission from those minds was lifted; all of them, who were mediums of vision and hearing, though unaware, now fully beheld the gift of mediumship revealed to them, making them fit to receive the Holy Spirit, that is, the pleiad of pure Spirits who would accompany them in the grand mission of spreading over the surface of the Earth the word of the GOSPEL — THE GOOD NEWS of salvation for all humanity.

And the Lord, some days later, by the shore of the Sea of Tiberias, seized the opportunity to obtain from Peter the reciprocal of his three denials, making him affirm three times, before His disciples, the love that he, the apostle of faith, bore for Him.

"Peter, do you love Me more than these?"

"Tend My lambs![73]"

Such were the words the Divine Lord addressed to the great apostle, the head of His Church, revealing His desire that Peter also participate in the labors intended to guide the first steps of Christianity.

"Peter, head of My Church, for love of Me, for love of My doctrine, I place the great fold of the world in your hands! Watch zealously over the flock of souls, for I go to the Father!

"For love of My doctrine, take up your pilgrim's staff and go, at the

---

[73] John, Chapter XXI, verses 1 to 17

head of My beloved disciples, opening those furrows of salvation, those new paths unknown to Gentiles and heretics! Teach all those poor outcasts, confined to life in these earthly prisons, everything you have heard from My lips; tell them of all the marvelous events you witnessed, of all My anguish, which you also shared out of love for Me, so that the time may come for this world to become what it cannot yet be — My true kingdom!

"And," speaking to His disciples, the Divine Master breathed upon their heads, saying to them: "Receive the Holy Spirit" — thus investing them with every power to fulfill their sacred mission.

Yet because he was not there when these events occurred, Thomas, upon returning to the fellowship of his friends, and learning that the Lord had been among them, expressed his disbelief, sharing that sad sentiment that overwhelms humanity — doubt in the power of God, who manifests Himself throughout all Nature in a grand and extraordinary manner, yet cannot be seen or touched, given humankind's pride and vanity.

Thomas erred; he was weak; but because of that weakness, he could not be cast out of the holy gathering; thus, filled with mercy and forgiveness, the Lord arranged to be seen once again by His disciples, in Thomas's presence.

Taking up His fluidic body again, the same that had served to quench the scribes' and Pharisees' thirst for blood, the Lord gave Thomas His hands to touch, and, opening His tunic slightly, showed him His wounds, so that the weak disciple might overcome his disbelief.

Bathed in tears, he fell at the Divine Master's feet, exclaiming: "My God and my Lord!"

"Blessed are those who have not seen and yet believed," the Gentle Lamb said to him[74]!

And we repeat: blessed are those who did not have the bittersweet fortune to witness the scenes in Palestine, yet believe in the evangelists' accounts and in the confirmation brought by the Lord's Messengers!

Blessed are the true Christians who have never trodden those lands nor had the joy of hearing the Savior of the world's words, but still believe in them; and because of that faith, raise from the depths of their souls the incense of prayers that ascend to the sidereal regions, to bear witness to the gentle Son of the Immaculate Virgin that the seeds He scattered have flourished in good soil, where they bloom and release

---

[74] John, Chapter XX, verses 24 to 29.

sweet fragrances worthy of mingling with the pure aromas the holy women carried to His sepulcher!

Blessed are all those who, before the splendors of the Universe, do not need to touch God, nor Our Lord Jesus Christ, to consider themselves creatures of the Most High!

And what a sad and terrible contrast! While the Divine Master strived to instill faith, courage, and ardor into the hearts of His beloved disciples, that they might spread the sweet and ripe fruits of His holy doctrine everywhere, far off, the representatives of the law were bribing the soldiers' conscience, prompting them with a foul lie, so that in the eyes of the people — astonished by the Lord's resurrection — that prodigious event, attesting to His divine authority, might pass off as some deception craftily arranged by His disciples[75]!

They had absolutely no interest in letting the people be convinced by yet another miracle, one that elevated the name of the Martyr of Golgotha to the divine heights from which He had descended.

Truth, however, was bound to prevail, and, despite that dark tragedy, His resurrection soon became evident to all who wished to see it, as the Divine Master, the Son of the living God on Earth.

For many days, Jesus visited His disciples, encouraging and strengthening them for the mission He had ordained for them, until the time came for Him to leave the surface of the Earth and ascend to the heights of light. He asked them to gather on a mountain in Galilee, where, after speaking His final words of encouragement and comfort, blessing them, that Sun of Love rose into the heavens, up to the feet of His Divine Father, leaving on Earth the valiant heralds who were to carry His sweet and divine word everywhere[76].

How these holy men carried out the sacred mission entrusted to them is well known to Christendom from the witness of the New Testament, and all humanity abundantly knows, from history, how those who succeeded them would later act!

The doctrine of Jesus, spread everywhere by His beloved disciples, then became a stumbling stone before upright, pure consciences.

By deliberately distorting the basic principles of the Gospel, discarding the purity and sanctity of the Lord's Code to favor only worldly interests, they lit the fires of persecution, devised the most appalling tortures, and, in the name of Jesus, the successors of the Beloved Lamb's disciples committed the greatest atrocities, carrying

---

[75] Matthew, Chapter XXVIII, verses 11 to 15.
[76] Mark, Chapter XVI, verse 19.

fire, destruction, and dishonor wherever they went!

As if that vast mass of criminal practices, which plunged the Gospel into a swamp of blood and treated Divinity with scorn, was not enough, the Christian family was summoned to worship idols, true inquisitorial murderers who, by human will, were exalted to the rank of saints!

And Christendom bore that heavy yoke without freedom of thought or freedom to feel, obliged to a passive obedience like that of slaves — all by the imposition of those whose duty was to enlighten its conscience, giving it the full enjoyment of the liberty that is an emanation of God!

Printing presses were established, not to spread the sweet, saving word of the gentle Nazarene to souls locked in deathlike slumber, nor to revive in writing the seeds sown by Our Lord Jesus Christ's blessed hands, but to sow hatred, slander, and persecution, that entire vile compendium that drives people to despair in the mire of Earth.

And in the name of Jesus, bishops of the Church were seen leading armor-clad armies, not to console the wretched who collapsed on the battlefield, kindling in them, at least, the sweet, comforting hope of mercy from their Divine Redeemer, but to spur them on to fight, igniting their thirst for blood, and not the blood of barbarian peoples — which would still be unjustifiable — but of cultured peoples defending their freedoms!

Well then, faced with this horrific scene, which we have briefly described to Christendom, the Consoler has come forward — the spirit of reform that descends to Earth by divine will, saying:

"Enough blood, enough hypocrisy, enough mire! Rise up! Come open this sacred book, whose shining pages have been hidden from your sight for centuries!

"Come learn the whole truth that was hidden from you, all the light that was stolen from your hearts and eyes!

"Come learn to love the Son of God, Our Lord Jesus Christ, with the love of a true believer, not in the mountains of Jerusalem nor dazzled by your grand cathedrals, but rather within your own hearts, which you shall make into a tabernacle by practicing the Divine Lamb's teachings, the only teachings that uplift the soul, preparing it to receive the Envoys of the Eternal!"

***

Thus, the Consoler is in fact upon the earth — Spiritism. And you,

Spiritists, laborers of the eleventh hour, permit the humblest servant of the Lord to call your attention to the responsibilities weighing upon your shoulders.

Remember that, just as the Church distorted the Beloved Master's teachings, it is also possible someone may attempt to distort the teachings of the Spiritist Doctrine, which is a reflection of the Divine Code.

Keep vivid in your minds the parable of the virgins in the Gospel of Matthew[77].

Consider that, just as the House of God was turned into a market for sacraments and indulgences, it is also possible that some of those claiming to be spiritists may seek to make of their workshop a means for satisfying personal interests!

But woe to those who behave so!

Far better had they never read that book of salvation, far better had they never understood God!

Spiritists, remember that Jesus has chosen you to restore the truths He proclaimed on Earth.

They are a splendid treasure that, like a precious pearl, lay hidden from humankind; you have discovered it. Therefore, buy with the price of your virtues the field in which it lies, and never abandon it, for Jesus relies on the sincerity of the faith you profess, trusting that you will know how to use that treasure for your salvation and for that of all His flock on Earth!

Whether you are mediums or not, strive always to stay in contact with your Guides, so that you may receive from them the inspiration for what you should do each day, to hasten the establishment of Jesus's reign on Earth, which is that of peace and love!

Banish from your soul all self-interest and selfishness, and remain vigilant so that, under no pretext, money may enter your workshop!

If you are mediums, prescribing remedies or healing, give freely what you have freely received; following the sacred path of the true disciples of Our Lord Jesus Christ, prepare your soul to accept any sacrifice for humankind!

Just as the first Christians willingly underwent all manner of suffering, singing hosannas to the holy name of Jesus, endeavor to stand firm with the full courage of your faith and conviction in that dire onslaught that will soon occur, for the time has come for Rome to fall, for the rule of the Gospel to prevail.

---

[77] Matthew, Chapter XXV, verses 1 to 13.

Such are the bitter fruits of human evil: after nineteen centuries of struggle, the reasoning world now beholds this dreadful spectacle — Rome cannot reconcile itself with the Gospel, nor can the Gospel reconcile itself with Rome!

Religion, declares the Syllabus, cannot conform to progress!

Nevertheless, so must it be. Progress is an eternal law presiding over the destinies of peoples by the influence of God's will; it results from the study and practice of Our Lord Jesus Christ's teachings, which denounce the pitfalls of obscurantism.

Progress has its origin and its end in the Bible[78]; and, tragically, human wickedness extends so far as to induce the ignorant masses to regard this sacred noun as an expression of offense, insult, and disdain.

The New Testament, in addition to the four Gospels of Matthew, Mark, Luke, and John, contains the Acts of the Apostles, the fourteen epistles of Paul, James, Peter, John, and Jude, and Revelation.

Hence, religion indeed cannot reconcile itself with progress, for Rome is the seat of falsehood, whereas the Gospel is the seat of truth, in which all progress is possible!

But we have finally reached the end of this painful journey: enough hypocrisy, enough treachery!

And you, Spiritists, legions of the new revelation, strong as lions in faith, and gentle in love like doves, come raise before sleeping consciences the cross of Golgotha!

And, pointing it out to your brothers, say to them:

"Prodigal children of heaven's great treasures, behold the symbol of love that was hidden from your sight! Love one another! Behold the most sacred cross — the symbol of humility — on which the purest of all Spirits who ever descended to Earth died for love of you: the Lamb of God! Be humble! In your consciences, establish the worship of justice and duty, which is the worship of the Lord; cast off your worldly

---

[78] From bíblos, biblion, meaning book: name given to the book containing the Sacred Scriptures. It is divided into two parts — the Old and New Testaments. The first part comprises the history of the people of God up to the birth of Our Lord Jesus Christ, containing: the five books of the Law or the Pentateuch of Moses — Genesis, Exodus, Leviticus, Numbers, and Deuteronomy; — Joshua, Judges, Ruth; the four books of Kings, Paralipomena; Ezra and Nehemiah; Esther, Job, Psalms, Proverbs, Ecclesiastes; the Song of Songs; the Prophecies of Isaiah, Jeremiah, Ezekiel, and Daniel; the book of the twelve prophets: Hosea, Joel, Amos, Obadiah, Jonah, Micah, Nahum, Habakkuk, Zephaniah, Haggai, Zechariah, and Malachi.

prejudices and come to the great vineyard to cultivate the seeds of the Gospel, for in that lies your salvation and your future happiness!"

That is how you should speak to Christendom, in the forceful language of a true believer, for the times are at hand and it is your duty to fulfill the mission granted to you: to raise from its ruins and dust that code of salvation — the Gospel of Jesus — which was cast aside by the Church of Rome.

Fools and dreamers they will call you, without a doubt; but do not be shaken by such labels. Take up your arms, the arms of the Gospel, and, undaunted, enter the fray, for victory shall be yours, victory shall be the truth's! Fools and dreamers!

That is what Rome called Galileo[79], through the Inquisition's voice, the founder of experimental physics! And as a fool and dreamer, he was delivered to martyrdom because he explained the biblical passage of Joshua[80] with his armies coming to the Gibeonites' aid as being caused by luminous fluids, giving the appearance of daylight long gone, accompanying him in order for him to achieve victory. Yet the scientific principle the martyr set forth prevailed, supported by human science; and there also remains the religious truth, supported by the New Revelation, which we can now understand by the mercy of Our Lord Jesus Christ and through our humble efforts to investigate the divine.

In 1633, he was denounced before the Inquisition tribunal in Rome, charged with contradicting the Bible in a published work that proved the Earth's movement and the Sun's immobility. Found guilty, he was forced to recant his doctrines and deprived of his liberty for a long time.

It is said that after recanting, he murmured under his breath: "Nevertheless, it moves."

Galileo was truly the founder of experimental physics, and many important scientific discoveries are owed to him.

His principal works include: Sidereus Nuntius, on astronomy;

---

[79] A native of Pisa, from a noble but poor family, he devoted himself to medicine and then to mathematical sciences. He spent some time as a professor at the University of his native city and later in Padua and Florence.

[80] Leader of the Hebrew people; he was Moses's successor and led the Hebrews into the Promised Land. He crossed the Jordan River and took possession of Jericho, whose walls he caused to fall to the sound of trumpets, and at Gibeon he defeated the allied five kings; during the battle, God made the sun stand still to prolong the day, allowing him to achieve victory.

Dialogues on the systems of Ptolemy and Copernicus; Dialogues on the movement and resistance of fluids, and various others. He died blind in 1642.

Joshua spent six years conquering the land of Canaan, dividing it among the twelve tribes. The Bible contains a book that bears his name and recounts his story.

Fools and dreamers, engage in the struggle between light and darkness, certain that, from on high, Jesus, the Divine Master, pours out the glorious radiance of His love upon you, blessing you for the efforts you make to reclaim the truths of His holy doctrine!

I urge you, however, to keep always in your memory Matthew, Chapter XXIV, for false Christians and false prophets shall arise, merchants of the temple who will seek to penetrate your battlefield to stab you in the back!

And by observing in all their purity and integrity the divine teachings of the Beloved Master's Code, offer to Christendom, through your actions, an example of virtue, so that they may see Jesus, understand their duties, and be guided toward that life where all is light, where all is love and happiness for those who cherish in their souls the love of God and love for their neighbor!

***

And to You, oh my Jesus, my Lord and my Divine Master! Thank You! You granted me the grace of being able to finish my task, a meager proof of my love for Your Holy Doctrine! If not for Your mercy, Your infinite love, this work — meant only to show Christendom Your holy and divine image — would have been left unfinished!

Allow, Lord, that they may understand me!

Grant that this book, traveling the world, may awaken in souls the love for studying the Gospel! May it be a light of hope, showing that not all is lost, and that, after so many struggles and so much ingratitude, it is still possible to find, upon the tranquil, gentle sea of Your holy doctrine, the boat of Your beloved Peter, bearing You, oh my divine Jesus, as its helmsman!

Thank You, Lord!

LAST WORDS

Still under the impression of the grand phenomenon now shaking the world — communication with the dead by the living, and in our case, more than grand, as it concerns not mere communications such as we are used to, but the gracious gift of a book, a reliquary of divine beauties and wonders — we, the small and humble believers in the New Revelation, come here to add our feeble word to that of the inspired Spirit who, in luminous language and thought, has engraved in this priceless work the image of Jesus, not as the Roman Church presents Him, but as He truly is, in His exalted and divine majesty.

We can add nothing to this book, whose intellectual and moral structure can withstand the test of ages. Yet we can testify that it was dictated mediumistically by the Spirit who, during his lifetime, was the notable Christian poet, Dr. Francisco Leite de Bittencourt Sampaio. And our testimony is true.

Let men of letters determine, by that principle that style is the man, whether The Divine Epopee and this present volume do not reveal the identity of their author, with the same certainty that in reading The Legend of the Ages, one may swear it is the work of the writer of *Les Orientales*[81].

Nor should one suppose, simply because the work was written via mediumship, that it is the mere outcome of transmitted thought. We solemnly affirm that none of us present, including the medium, possess the capacity needed to produce a monument that, in both style and thought, challenges the most celebrated authors of all time.

Hence, faced with this twofold proof, only the most astute bad faith

---

[81] Translator's note: "The Orientals", a collection of poems by Victor Hugo (1829).

or the most abysmal ignorance — both equally lamentable in matters of this nature — could deny the author of The Divine Epopee, written by Bittencourt Sampaio during his lifetime, the authorship of Jesus Before Christendom, dictated by Bittencourt Sampaio after his death.

Evidently, these are two leaves from the same tree — two petals from the same flower — twin brothers, unmistakably attesting to their paternal origin.

On this subject, we say no more.

***

This masterwork did not arrive unexpectedly. In what was published in 1896, titled *Trabalhos Espíritas*[82], edited by Antônio Luiz Sayão, there appears a noteworthy communication, received mediumistically, regarding the struggle — now more intense than ever — between defenders of the evangelical truths in their spiritual purity and those on Earth and beyond who reject or distort them for their own interests and passions.

In that most salient essay, the high Spirit who authored it vehemently stressed the need for all who wish to be true disciples of Jesus to unite, so that the pure spiritual doctrine of the Gospel might be restored and firmly established.

And to secure that blessed goal, he promised to dictate a book that would present Our Lord Jesus Christ before humanity in the historical light of Christianity.

That promise was faithfully fulfilled by him who made it: our former companion in these works, Bittencourt Sampaio, a name graced with fame in politics, which would have been his shirt of Nessus had he not, in good time, cast it off, renouncing worldly glory for a burning desire to know divine things, to which — and especially to studying the Gospel in the light of Spiritism — he dedicated all the powers of his soul.

The vessel that raised the white Faith banner, sparkling with the radiant beams of Truth — which is Jesus, of Jesus — which is life, of life — which is the glorification of the Supreme Creator, did not sail upon calm waters like a sea of roses.

The prince of darkness, still lord of this world, could not remain indifferent to an undertaking that, by enlarging the sphere of the truth's light, forced the boundaries of his grievous domain to retreat.

---

[82] Translator's note: "Spiritist Works"

And he summoned, in fury, all the powers of evil, hurling himself against the humble believers, confident that he could stifle their progress and thwart the venture he detested.

Many times we were attacked by these wretches with a ferocity worthy of those convinced they would annihilate us all.

Yet God, who allowed them to use their power fully, in order to prove that evil can never triumph over good, shielded us with the mantle of His mercy. The dark hordes were repelled in their accursed effort, and the small and weak continued to receive the manna from Heaven brought by Bittencourt Sampaio.

Glory to the Father and to the Son, who granted us the grace of providing, for the starving, this white bread of His most holy charity!

Thanks to Bittencourt Sampaio, who, knowing the frailties of his old companions, obtained from Jesus for them the gift of light, this book — which shows them the way, opens their eyes to the many errors beclouding human reason, and bestows the strength of the reasoned faith by which they shall cast aside the mountains of their own iniquities.

In the name of the Queen of Angels, peace to the workers of goodwill, mercy to all who suffer the consequences of their errors, here on Earth as well as beyond.

August — 1898.

Adolfo Bezerra de Menezes
Frederico Pereira da Silva Júnior
Antônio Luiz Sayão
Luiz Antônio dos Santos
Pedro Richard
José Antônio de Mattos Cid
Tiago Bevilacqua
José Dias de Carvalho Neto
João Augusto Ramos da Silveira
José Luiz de Almeida
José Augusto Ramos da Silveira
Cândido José de Abrantes
Pedro Luiz de Oliveira Sayão

ABOUT THE AUTHORS

Francisco Leite de Bittencourt Sampaio

LIFE

Francisco Leite de Bittencourt Sampaio was born on February 1, 1834, in Laranjeiras, in the province of Sergipe, Brazil. He was the son of a Portuguese merchant, also named Francisco Leite de Bittencourt Sampaio, and of Maria de Sant'Ana Leite Sampaio. From a young age, he displayed an aptitude for study and critical thought—traits that would guide him through a multifaceted career as a legal scholar, magistrate, political figure, journalist, poet, and prominent participant in Brazil's early Spiritist movement.

Bittencourt Sampaio first enrolled at the Law School in Recife, but in 1856, his studies were briefly disrupted when he devoted himself to caring for those stricken by a cholera epidemic in Pernambuco. The Imperial Government recognized his humanitarian service by awarding

him the Order of the Rose—an honor he refused due to his firmly held political convictions. He resumed his legal education in São Paulo and graduated in 1859, thereafter serving as a public prosecutor in the towns of Itabaiana and Laranjeiras.
Seeking broader professional opportunities, Bittencourt Sampaio moved to Rio de Janeiro in March 1861. There, he practiced law and became involved in the Liberal Party, winning election to the Chamber of Deputies in two consecutive terms (1864–1866 and 1867–1870). During his second term, he was appointed President (governor) of Espírito Santo, serving from September 29, 1867, to April 26, 1868, after which he returned to his legislative role. By 1870, moved by ideals of republican governance, he left the Liberal Party and became one of the signatories of the "Manifesto of December 3, 1870," a pivotal document advocating for the establishment of a republic in Brazil.
Following the proclamation of the Republic in 1889, Bittencourt Sampaio was commissioned to assess and organize the archives of the former Imperial Chamber of Deputies and later served as a recorder of debates during the Constituent Assembly. His experience and stature led to his appointment as the first Director of the National Library in Rio de Janeiro to bear that official title, reflecting his commitment to public service and intellectual development.
Bittencourt Sampaio passed away on October 10, 1895, at the age of 61. Accounts from those who knew him describe him as consistently joyful and warmly disposed toward all who crossed his path.

SPIRITISM
Although it is not certain when Bittencourt Sampaio embraced Spiritism, by August 2, 1873, he was already part of the governing board of "Group Confucius," considered the first Spiritist society in Rio de Janeiro. There, he honed his healing mediumship, dispensing homeopathic remedies and immersing himself in the study of mediumistic phenomena. Nevertheless, what most profoundly touched him was the moral dimension of Spiritism, which likewise inspired his founding of the "Society for Spiritist Studies God, Christ and Charity" in 1876. He played an active role in subsequent Spiritist initiatives, including contributing to the "Spiritist Society Fraternity," founded in 1880.
Bittencourt Sampaio's literary output includes "The Divine Epopee of John Evangelist," published in 1882, an original rendering of the Gospel of John in decasyllabic verse—an unprecedented endeavor in world literature. This work also comprised extensive prose

commentaries explaining each canto through the lens of Spiritist doctrine. At the time of his passing in 1895, he was preparing a follow-up project titled "The Divine Tragedy of the Golgotha." Posthumously, through the medium Frederico Pereira da Silva Júnior, Bittencourt Sampaio produced several notable works, including the current work, "Jesus Before Christendom", and others, such as, "From Jesus to the Children," and "From the Calvary to the Apocalypse," further cementing his legacy as an influential proponent of Spiritist thought.

Even after his death, Spiritist literature portrays Bittencourt Sampaio as continuing his mission in the higher realms, guiding and supervising the Spiritist movement in Brazil. His life and work remain a testament to profound dedication, blending legal acumen, political engagement, literary achievement, and spiritual conviction in service of both country and faith.

Frederico Pereira da Silva Júnior

LIFE

Frederico Pereira da Silva Junior was born in 1857, in Rio de Janeiro, Brazil. He was raised among humble workers and, despite the many temptations of the bohemian life so common at the time, he maintained a docile personality and a reputation as a kind-hearted man. Friends and colleagues alike admired him for his good nature and readiness to render assistance to those in need.

Despite possessing limited formal instruction, he showed remarkable intelligence. Professionally, Frederico served as a public employee at the General Post Office. Over the course of his life, he married twice, became a widower after his first marriage, and had children in both unions.

Though never seeking the limelight, Frederico's natural goodness and sense of duty endeared him to his contemporaries. Close friends witnessed his constant willingness to help, combined with a remarkable resilience in facing the adversities that life placed before him.

He battled various personal struggles, including difficult emotional trials that tested his fortitude and faith. Yet he also found profound solace and meaning through his wholehearted dedication to charitable works—efforts that would sustain him during many of the challenges he faced.

In the final years of his life, Frederico developed tuberculosis, which he fought with unwavering conviction. On August 30, 1914, at home in Rio de Janeiro, he gathered his family around him and offered a solemn prayer dedicated to Mary of Nazareth. The moment he finished praying, he passed away quietly, leaving a legacy of service and devotion that continues to inspire.

SPIRITISM

Frederico's greater involvement with Spiritism began in 1878, when he was 21 years old. At the invitation of his godfather, he visited the "Society for Spiritist Studies God, Christ and Charity", hoping to receive information regarding someone dear to him. During his attendance, he experienced a powerful spiritual influence and soon began to work as a medium in the séances—a role that would define much of his life's work.

Gifted with several distinct mediumistic abilities, Frederico practiced psychophony (including somnambulic trance), psychography, clairvoyance, clairaudience, healing, and even physical phenomena. From 1878 to 1880, he offered his services at the God, Christ and Charity Society and from 1880 to 1882 at the "Spiritist Society Fraternity". Yet most of his 34 years of uninterrupted spiritist activity would take place within the renowned "Ismael Spiritist Society", later absorbed into Brazilian Spiritist Federation (FEB). There, he labored alongside prominent pioneers of Spiritism in Brazil, including Adolfo Bezerra de Menezes, Antônio Luiz Sayão, Francisco Leite de Bittencourt Sampaio, and Pedro Richard.

The breadth of Frederico's mediumistic gifts is attested by well-respected figures in the Spiritist movement. In the book "The Tragedy of Saint Mary," the spirit Bezerra de Menezes, through the mediumship of Yvonne do Amaral Pereira, describes Frederico as a man of "exquisite moral qualities and vast psychic endowment," ranking him among the most significant mediums of all time. During Bezerra de Menezes's physical life, he relied on Frederico to convey valuable spiritual communications from Ismael, Celina (Mary of Nazareth's messenger), and other high-order spirits guiding the development of Spiritism within Brazil. In fact, just 24 hours after Bezerra's own passing in 1900, his spirit communicated through Frederico during a session at the Ismael Spiritist Society—offering words of consolation and hope to his friends still on Earth.

An equally remarkable episode occurred in 1889, when Allan Kardec's spirit, through Frederico's mediumship, transmitted specific guidance to Spiritist workers in Rio de Janeiro. Later recorded in "Brazil, Heart of the World, Homeland of the Gospel", this communication strongly emphasized harmonious unification, charity, and earnest study in support of the young movement.

Upon his passing on August 30, 1914, Frederico left behind not only a family but also a spiritual legacy that would continue. He is said to have "photographed in the ether" a final image of devotion to Mary of Nazareth, as he concluded his last prayer. From the spirit realm, he is confirmed to remain active in efforts to expand and reinforce Christian Spiritism, as attested by subsequent spirit communications and records—such as in the book "Voltei" (I'm Back), penned by the spirit "Brother Jacob" (Frederico Figner) and published by the FEB.

To this day, Frederico Pereira da Silva Junior's persistence, dedication, and deep love of service stand as shining examples for all those seeking to labor in the vineyard of the Spiritist cause—forever honoring Ismael's guiding motto of "God, Christ, and Charity."

Made in the USA
Columbia, SC
13 April 2025

d2aa05a0-47a2-424b-98bc-eac44a0c3e94R01